TIME PLANNING TOOLS AND TECHNIQUES

Learn How to Create Your Personal Time Planning and Discover the Most Efficient Tools and Techniques for Organizing Your Time, Cultivate Your Passions and Become The Master of Your Time.

By Scott Darley

Table of Contents

Introduction

There are differences in the manner a culture perspectives time and this can influence the manner in which they oversee or plan their time.

But what precisely is time planning or the management?

At the point when we talk about the way toward planning and practicing cognizant control of time spent on explicit exercises, particularly to build adequacy, proficiency, and profitability. It includes a shuffling demonstration of different requests upon an individual identifying with work, public activity, family, side interests, individual interests and responsibilities with the limit of time. Utilizing time viably gives the individual "decision" on spending/overseeing exercises at their own time and convenience. It is a meta-action with the objective to amplify the general advantage of a lot of different exercises inside the limit state of a constrained measure of time, as time itself can't be overseen in light of the fact that it is fixed. A scope of skills, devices, may help time the management and strategies used to oversee time when achieving explicit task, ventures, and objectives conforming to a due date. At first, time the management alluded to simply business or work exercises, yet in the long run the term widened to incorporate individual exercises too. A period the management framework is a structured blend of procedures, instruments, strategies, and techniques. Time the management is normally a need in any undertaking advancement as it decides the task finishing time and degree. It is likewise imperative to comprehend that both specialized and basic contrasts in time the management exist because of varieties in social ideas of time.

The significant subjects emerging from a few literary works on great time planning incorporates; the capacity to making a domain helpful for adequacy, setting of needs, and the related procedure of decrease of time spent on non-needs, and Usage of objectives. Time planning methodologies are frequently connected with the proposal to set individual objectives. Objective setting is additionally fundamental to oversee time effectively.

These objectives are recorded and might be separated into a venture, an activity plan, or a basic assignment list. For individual task or for objectives, a significance rating might be built up, cutoff times might be set, and needs doled out. This procedure brings about an arrangement with an undertaking list or a timetable or schedule of exercises. Creators may suggest a day by day, week after week, month to month, or other planning periods related with various extent of planning or survey. This is done in different manners as fit.

Have you heard of Pareto Analysis?

Pareto investigation is the possibility that 80% of errands can be finished in 20% of the expendable time, and the staying 20% of task will occupy 80% of the time. This guideline is utilized to sort task into two sections. As indicated by this type of Pareto investigation, it is prescribed that task that fall into the primary classification be appointed a higher need.

The 80-20-rule can likewise be applied to build profitability: it is expected that 80% of the efficiency can be accomplished by doing 20% of the errands. Thus, 80% of results can be ascribed to 20% of action. If profitability is the point of time the management, at that point these errands ought to be organized higher.

It relies upon the technique embraced to finish the undertaking. There is constantly a more straightforward and simpler approach to finish the undertaking. In the event that one uses a perplexing way, it will be tedious. In this way, one ought to consistently attempt to discover elective approaches to finish each errand.

Along these lines, in this digital book, I'll make you through all the stride, devices, procedures, and methods on the best way to design your time viably. You will thus utilize your time. Furthermore, this time, considerably more profitable than any time in recent memory. I will train you some close to home received systems what's more on how you can consolidate your profession, family, children, companions, and have a ton of fun filled public activity regardless you have extravagance of uninterrupted alone time. A few people would state; gracious 24 hours is too little for them, however that is all we have, that is every one of the Extremely rich people have as well, and each effective vocation lady and man have as well. In this way, the stuff is a successful time planning framework.

So sit back and read on as I unfurl these colossal secrets on time planning ...

Chapter 1
What Is Time Planning

For what reason is it so critical to manage our time in a correct manner? It is an outstanding idea that there is a tremendous scope of different variables that constitute our life, for example, work, family, companions, home, sport, contemplating and so forth. That is the reason the achievement we long for just as fulfillment and delight we gain from our life relies upon our capacity to deal with our time in a legitimate manner.

Have you at any point asked yourself, in what way can she/he think of such a significant number of targets she/he sets? In what manner can she/he be an ideal spouse/wife, a perfect dad/mother, solid and well off, find time for heading off to the moving school, perusing bunches of books, and still possess enough free energy for doing origami, doing every one of these objectives as a bit of cake? The appropriate response is shockingly basic: this supposed 'can-do-all individual' knows the mystery of impeccable time management, just as knows about how to apply the time arranging instruments.

Time - the worst waste of all

Everyone wastes things; there's no reason for arguing that. Indeed, even the most cautious, the most frugal individual will end up burning through something at some time sooner or later. With many people, it's not irregular to waste food, gas in the vehicle, and money   on a wide range of things.

What might you say is the greatest waste of all? Almost certainly, numerous things you buy and never use or despise the manner in which you figured you would may ring a bell. You may waste money on another phone that you never again find energizing after the main week or on link channels, you never watch. You may waste gas in your vehicle getting such a large number of things done when you could have and ought to have consolidated them in one. Maybe you wasted food by not using it before it turned sour or by cooking excessively and discarding the remains.

Be that as it may, with every one of the things that are wasted in one's life, most likely time is the greatest waste of all. individuals sit around on futile exercises that don't generally serve their needs or on obligations that are not done right the first run through. Time can be wasted from resting excessively, from accomplishing hurtful things like over drinking or utilizing narcotics, and from out and out sitting on the lounge chair staring at the TV.

Regularly time is wasted, not on the grounds that individuals enjoy exercises that could be viewed as a waste of time, but since of lack of foresight and time the management skills. You may compare this with how individuals waste money on food since they don't use it before it decays or in light of the fact that they cook excessively. In the event that an individual has better skills when it came to setting up that food and had the control expected to go through the food in the house before looking for additional, they may not see such a great amount of go down the trash. It's not their eating that is simply the issue in and obviously it's not the deficiency of the food that it spoils; it's the manner by which the food is arranged and utilized that makes a waste.

So it is with time the management skills. An individual may work, work, work, and wonder for what reason they're not completing anything. They may likewise sincerely feel that they don't indulge in time wasting exercises, for example, staring at the TV or going out with companions to the bar each night. However, for what reason would they say they are not achieving anything or arriving at the objectives they once had for themselves?

Typically, the issue is figuring out how to deal with one's time and to amplify it for the most viability. Much the same as figuring out how to cook and deal with one's shopping can mean better utilization of the food in the home with less waste, so figuring out how to be responsible for one's time and one's calendar can mean less time wasted.

Your allotment of time

Have you at any point wound up wishing there were more hours in the day in which you could work? Presumably along these lines, a great many people wish this at once or another. Between vocations, family errands, dealing with kids, and needing a smidgen of harmony and calm for yourself, almost certainly you've discovered sleep time showing up too early over and over.

But, has it at any point jumped out at you that individuals all around the earth are equivalent in the way that they all get a similar measure of time each and every day? This might be the one steady that everybody shares! You have 24 hours simply like your chief, your neighbor, the President, your preferred VIP, and gracious indeed, that individual that you respect since they generally appear to complete things viably.

Understanding that your time is limited and that you have a similar measure of time similarly as every other person does should assist you with understanding the significance of effective time management better. Why would that be? How about we again compare time with money. Individuals that are battling monetarily frequently expect that in the event that they simply made a couple of dollars more than they do today, at that point they wouldn't battle and would have every one of their bills paid, and would make an amazing time with their life.

Obviously, there are those that battle since they genuinely live in destitution and this isn't what we're thinking about here. The fact of the matter is that while it's enticing to imagine that the response to money issues is to have more money; this isn't generally the situation. Think about those that have truly a large number of dollars in their possession and still end up bowing out of all financial obligations or confronting different genuine money related issues. Almost certainly some VIP names ring a bell. Also, if these individuals who are making a huge number of dollars consistently still face money issues, what is the issue?

Clearly, the appropriate response is that it's the manner in which they deal with their money. Having more money won't help in the event that you spend it on futile things that lose esteem and if you don't put something aside for the future too. Those famous people and others that have a lot of money coming in yet who face insolvency and abandonment and these issues have not dealt with the money they have.

So it is with time. In the event that you had 50 hours in the day or even 100, who is to state that you would achieve more in that time. If you haven't figured out how to deal with the 24 you're designated, getting additional time most likely won't have a lot of effect in amplifying your calendar and accomplishing your objectives.

Once it's gone...

One major thought with regards to sitting around idly wasting time is that once it's gone, it's gone. At the point when you waste money, you can acquire more, when you waste food you can purchase more, etc. But, with time, there is no cycle of it that repurchases the time that is lost.

Indeed, you will have an additional 24 hours tomorrow however everybody's life is limited; the 24 hours you've wasted today is being subtracted from the absolute number of hours you'll have in your life generally. You can't recover those hours the manner in which you can renew your financial balance when you buy something pointless.

This also is the reason time is so valuable thus important. What's more, this is the reason wasting it is presumably one of the most noticeably awful things an individual can do! There is no making things the same as before and there is no real way to recover that time that is no more.

Time as an investment

Another motivation to think about how time is simply too valuable to even consider wasting is that it can likewise be viewed as an interest in one's future. The manner in which you invest your energy today has an impact on your conditions tomorrow.

At the point when you set goals and utilize your time toward accomplishing them, you can before long wind up living with the final product of those objectives being practiced.

Be that as it may, if you sit around idly and let your time waste, at that point you don't have anything to appear for it when tomorrow shows up. There are numerous ways this can be valid; consider a couple here:

- When you invest energy and time with your kids and family now, you are reinforcing family bonds that can endure forever. Your connections will be more grounded and everybody will feel nearer.
- Investing time in assisting your training can mean additionally gaining force. This may mean a progressively agreeable way of life, an increasingly secure retirement, and the capacity to accommodate oneself and one's family.
- Spending time today thinking about your wellbeing may mean less wellbeing worries later on. This may mean practicing progressively, setting aside the effort to plan solid foods, and things, for example, these.
- There are likewise numerous individual objectives you no uncertainty have that mean putting time so as to accomplish; If you don't contribute that time, you won't have the future you envision.

For example, assume you need to adopt a child. This implies examining the procedure, choosing a lawyer, setting up your home, and doing anything that else is important to be qualified for selection and to get it going. In the event that you don't utilize your time today to progress in the direction of that objective, obviously it will never simply occur!

8

Taking into account how time is an interest in your future ought to likewise urge you to figure out how to oversee it shrewdly. If you let it sneak away, this venture will never satisfy. However, If you use it to arrive at your objectives for tomorrow, at that point you're utilizing your speculation carefully.

Obviously, this is fine and dandy, however realizing how valuable time is doesn't ordinarily drive anybody to utilize it carefully. Pretty much anybody and everybody sits around idly regularly in their lives. Why would that be? What's more, how might you change this?

Let's first see why time is regularly wasted and afterward we can proceed onward to tending to how to fix these things.

Why is time being wasted?

If time is so valuable, significant, thus restricted, for what reason is it generally so wasted today? For what reason do individuals waste it, decline to perceive its worth, and neglect to figure out how to oversee it astutely?

The appropriate response will be diverse for everybody. The propensities you have that sit around idly wasting your time will not be quite the same as the practices another person has. The reasons you battle to deal with your time will be not the same as the reasons why your life partner is so disordered, in every case late, and never appears to achieve things either.

Normally, anyway there are some regular explanations behind time being wasted today, and for poor time the management skills. How about we investigate these normal reasons and afterward we can examine every one of them in more prominent detail.

The Pareto Principle

The Pareto Principle is a philosophy with respect to circumstances and logical results; it is additionally Sometimes called the eighty twenty principle. It basically expresses that all the time, 80% of the impact originates from 20% of the causes. For instance, of how this guideline may function in various conditions, assume an individual is overweight. Odds are most of their concern comes from a couple of little negative behavior patterns they have. At the end of the day, some 80% of their overabundance body weight is most likely there on account of 20% of their food decisions. Those additional treats they have or seared foods may make up just 20% of their day by day diet, yet they can most likely record for most of their overabundance weight.

As another model, assume family or individual faces monetary issues despite the fact that they make enough money to help themselves. It might just be that lone a couple of unfortunate propensities with regards to spending are answerable for most of their money related concerns. Along these lines, 20% of the things they do with their money are causing some 80% of the issues they have with it.

It even applies to business. In the event that you have a business, you look cautiously at the task, and which produce the most money, you will probably locate that 20% of the assignments you complete will create most of your profit. It is simply an issue .of working out which 20% is the most beneficial, and concentrating on those. Take a gander at the amount progressively beneficial you could be If you were placing your exertion into the correct territories.

Presently we should think about how this Principle may apply to time the management. Most likely, there are numerous things you should do for the duration of the day over which you have next to no say, and there are many time wasters that are simply part of the present world. Remaining in line, holding up at red lights, enduring one more meeting that your manager leads just to hear himself talk; these are time wasters however they're a part of the present life. To get where we need to go, to purchase the food and different things we need, to have a vocation and gain money, we should just endure these things.

Notwithstanding, with regards to decisions you make about your very own time, almost certainly, it's only a little bunch of unfortunate propensities, or a slight piece of fumble that records for most of the waste time in your life.

Think about how this may be valid. Only two hours of TV consistently at night means 14 hours in a week is wasted. That is nearly a similar measure of hours you go through during two days at work! One evening of running all over town to deal with tasks that you haven't sorted out into a fast outing can mean pretty much your whole day wasted, as you may then be too worn out to even consider doing whatever else by the day's end.

Regularly little propensities and little league wasters can indicate hours, days, weeks, and afterward years being wasted away. The key is to distinguish those propensities and afterward find a way to address them appropriately!

Procrastination

One normal component with regards to wasting time is Procrastination. We put off and put off those upsetting task or the work that is expected to achieve our objectives for whatever length of time that conceivable. Now and again, this may imply that in the end a circumstance deals with itself yet once in a while is that the case. As a Principle, we make more issues for ourselves when we put off work or anything that else is essential in our conditions. One reason that Procrastination is such a period waster is, that the time is sitting in that spot before us, yet we don't do anything with it. As opposed to utilize it to achieve our objectives we simply let it sneak away. As stated, when it's gone, it's away for good. Moreover, dawdling doesn't generally cause the issue to leave. Despite everything we have to adjust the checkbook and get ourselves on track monetarily, get that training, get another line of work, get out the upper room, etc. Because we won't accomplish these things, that doesn't mean they don't have to complete! Stalling does simply defer the unavoidable.

Interruptions

You would believe that Interruptions would do little to make you waste time. All things considered, when the Interruptions is over you can essentially return to what you were doing, isn't that so?

Actually, Interruptions can meddle with time the management in a couple of ways. One is that we misplace our thought process. At the point when we're hindered and afterward come back to our work, we regularly need to survey where we were and what we were thinking at the time. We have to help ourselves to remember the bearing in which we were going. At times we even overlook what we were attempting to achieve out and out!

Interruptions can likewise mean losing enthusiasm for the main job and this can mean putting it off. What we figured we would achieve today gets set aside for later on the grounds that something different has come up, and soon we simply couldn't care less to proceed by any means.

Lack of goals

Sometimes individual doesn't invest their time viably on the grounds that they don't know what they ought to do with that time. Without clear goals in mind, it's anything but difficult to just waste away an amazing hours doing little to achieve anything - on the grounds that you don't have a clue what you need to achieve.

Goals can be close to home or proficient, and huge or little. Having them as a top priority implies knowing where you need to be later on, and can assist you with seeing the things you have to do to arrive. For instance, if one goal is to set aside quite a lot of money for retirement, you realize that you have to maintain your accounts in control now and need to perceive the amount you're sparing each month. If a smaller goal is to wipe out your upper room, you may realize that this implies getting some trash sacks and capacity canisters and putting aside time each week to handle that undertaking.

At the point when you lack goals, it's very easy to lack focus. focus you have no clue how you ought to invest your time, which thusly implies you don't achieve anything.

No Prioritizing

Absence of prioritizing skills is something like lacking goal in that you don't have a clue what ought to involve the time you have for most extreme viability. You have a wide range of requests on your time and inability to acknowledge which should start things out and which should come last, and which ought to be dropped from your schedule inside and out, can mean burning through that valuable time.

Not prioritizing with your schedule can be compared with not organizing with your funds. If you purchase new garments without paying your lease, you have your needs befuddled. In the event that you go out drinking with your companions or go betting instead of sending in a vehicle installment, obviously your needs are off!

Figuring out how to set needs may mean figuring out how to disapprove of specific task or requests. This can be troublesome particularly for those that are not used to turning down solicitations and requests on their time, however like other time management skills, it very well may be finished.

Delegating

Do you delegate your work, regardless of whether that is work in the workplace or work at home? In the event that you make some troublesome memories with this, you're unquestionably not the only one. Many battle with allocating work or sharing duties, and for different reasons. It may be that they feel they're the main ones that can deal with the work, they nit-pick and condemn crafted by others, they figure others will look down on them If they share their duties, or they simply don't have a clue how to request help.

Whatever the explanation, taking on a lot of for the most part implies that something if not all things will endure. It additionally implies that the things that are essential to you may not be thought about since there is little room in your timetable for them.

These diverse time wasters and time desperados are extremely basic for some. Almost certainly you've seen yourself in a portion of these situations. Furthermore, provided that this is true, what at that point? How might you address these circumstances with the goal that you can augment your time and truly consider it your own?

Chapter 2
Planning Techniques

With every one of the obligations heaped on entrepreneurs, it is no big surprise that they wish for additional time, a progressively composed business process or expanded open doors for arranging. With the correct arrangement, organization and time management techniques, you can make an increasingly proficient and gainful working environment. A few procedures are effectively executed. Others take longer, however you may find that it merits the expanded organization not far off.

Planning Techniques

Planning is a fundamental component of maintaining a business used to address potential difficulties before they surface. Planning can limit transportation costs, decide the most proficient approaches to dole out occupations, decide planning needs, distinguish assets and new markets, and facilitate huge scale ventures. One Planning method is to endeavor to evaluate vulnerabilities, for example, request changes or gear breakdowns by foreseeing their probability and creating methodologies to counteract or beat these difficulties. Key Planning is another business strategy that enables entrepreneurs to recognize present moment and long haul objectives, and afterward creating steps to coordinate the organization toward those objectives. A few organizations use looking into as a Planning procedure, assessing the organization's past exhibitions to imitate or surpass its triumphs and maintain a strategic distance from its stumbles.

Organization Techniques

Organized businesses have spurred, productive staffs, as per More Business, an online business asset. Select a strategy for fulfilling and rousing representatives that supplements your business style and utilize this to compensate champion conduct. Keeping the workplace or business customer facing facade slick by setting normally utilized things on display and dispensing with mess is another organization method. Making installments on schedule, consistently invoicing clients and keeping convenient business arrangements all mean a composed business. PCs are powerful business organization apparatuses for bookkeeping, stock, and planning conveyances to keep away from blunder and give simple to-get to computerized copies.

Planning and assessment are fundamental for organization s. Planning is a procedure of choosing ahead of time, where we need to get to (our goals) and how we will arrive. Assessment empowers us to evaluate how well we are getting along and to gain from this.

This guide is composed for non-profit organizations that play a formative or administration job. Planning and assessment are especially significant for these organization s since they exist to make a noteworthy commitment to society:

- Planning encourages us to choose what that commitment ought to be and how to accomplish it.
- Evaluation empowers us to pass judgment on whether we have had the effect, we arranged, added to changing the circumstance we needed to change, and whether we accomplished our objective.

How to ensure planning is useful and contributes to effective results

There are six fundamental issues that are imperative to recollect about how Planning is finished. These will assist you with ensuring your Planning addresses the difficulties sketched out above, evades normal issues and that your arrangements are valuable and successful.

Planning and assessment must be participative. Everybody who must make a key commitment to work by the organization ought to be incorporated. There are two key purposes behind this. Firstly, it empowers you to draw on various thoughts and experience to settle on better choices. Besides, it enables you to fabricate responsibility to these choices by including every one of the individuals who should add to the fruitful execution of the Planning choices. Support will guarantee that everybody completely comprehends the system and designs and are focused on accomplishing the choices that have been made. You should distinguish and investigate every key partner that can influence whether you accomplish your motivation and choose whether and how they ought to be incorporated.

Planning and evaluation must be systematic. You need to guarantee you have thoroughly considered and concurred on every single key issue before proceeding onward to the subsequent stage. For instance, you should be clear about the outcomes you expect to accomplish before you start settling on choices about what move you will make. Non- profit organization s exists to have any kind of effect to society, not simply to get things done. All that you do must be pertinent to the outcomes you mean to accomplish. You may likewise once in a while need to move back to past strides in the Planning procedure, if the later Planning proposes you have to reevaluate some previous choices. For instance, you may understand that the activity you would should have the option to take isn't practical. This may lead you to conclude that you should adjust your choices about what results you can reasonably hope to accomplish. Successful Planning only from time to time moves in a single straight line yet this doesn't mean it ought not to be precise.

All planning should be strategic. This implies you should use your Planning pro processes cedars to locate the most ideal methods for having any kind of effect and the best way to deal with doing this. Every conceivable option ought to be analyzed, not simply the ones we are alright with. Viable Planning lays the reason for continuous vital thinking and activity from everybody who will add to accomplishing your organization's motivation. All choices and activity and all utilization of assets need to cause the vital commitment to accomplishing the reason you to have concurred on.

Planning must include agreements about how and when you will evaluate progress and achievements. You should settle on choices about what you will use to let you know whether you are gaining ground or have accomplished your motivation. You will likewise need to concur on where you will get the information, when you will assess, how, and who ought to be included.

Effective planning requires a major commitment from everyone in the organization. Planning can require some serious energy; it can appear to be chaotic and baffling. Notwithstanding, thinks about show that one of the key factors in viable Planning is the means by which submitted the organization and the individuals are to the Planning procedure. A further key factor here is that enough time ought to be given to Planning viably – it will spare you time later.

Planning and evaluation must be thought of as a cycle of learning and improvement, not a straight line from A to B We should ceaselessly assess what we are accomplishing and utilize our figuring out how to grow increasingly powerful methods for accomplishing our objectives.

Recognizing the Advantages of Planning

The military saying, "If you fail to plan, you plan to fail," is valid. Without proper planning, managers are set up to experience mistakes, waste, and delays. A plan, then again, enables a manager to sort out assets and exercises proficiently and viably to accomplish objectives.

The benefits of Planning are various. Planning satisfies the following targets:

Gives an organization a sense of direction. Without plans and goals, organizations only respond to every day events without thinking about what will occur over the long haul. For instance, the arrangement that bodes well in the present moment doesn't generally bode well in the long haul. Plans maintain a strategic distance from this float circumstance and guarantee that short-range endeavors will bolster and blend with future objectives.

Focuses attention on objectives and results. Plans keep the individuals who complete them concentrated on the foreseen outcomes. Moreover, keeping sight of the objective likewise inspires workers.

Establishes a basis for teamwork. Various bunches can't viably collaborate in joint projects without an incorporated plan. Example are: Handymen, woodworkers, and circuit repairmen can't construct a house without diagrams. What's more, military exercises require the coordination of Armed force, Naval force, and air armed forces units.

Helps anticipate problems and cope with change. When the management plans, it can help estimate future issues and roll out any essential improvements in advance to stay away from them. Obviously, shocks —, for example, the 1973 quadrupling of oil costs — can generally get an organization short, yet numerous progressions are simpler to gauge. Making arrangements for these potential issues, limits botches and lessen the "shocks" that definitely happen.

Provides guidelines for decision-making. Choices are future-oriented. In the event that administration doesn't have any designs for the future, they will have not many rules for settling on current choices. In the event that an organization realizes that it needs to present another item three years later on, its administration must be aware of the choices they make now. Plans help the two administrators and representatives keep their eyes on the comprehensive view.

Serves as a prerequisite to employing all other management functions. Planning is essential, in light of the fact that without recognizing what an organization needs to achieve, the board can't insightfully attempt any of the other fundamental administrative exercises: sorting out, staffing, driving, and additionally controlling.

Planning and business

Planning is basic to the accomplishment of any business. At the point when an organization has a plan to pursue, leaders are better prepared to plan for what's to come. A business plan makes a focus for the company, joining representatives toward shared goals. At the point when everybody cooperates, it's simpler to oversee time and assets, to situate the organization for development.

Set Goals

Planning enables a business to recognize its objectives. Planning for the future enables business pioneers to consider the effect they might want the organization to have and to figure out how to arrive. At the point when a group cooperates to set objectives, it enables everybody to be in agreement, moving in the direction of a typical, shared reason. Laborers are better ready to perceive approaches to work to accomplish objectives, just as practices to keep away from that could keep the organization from arriving at its destinations.

Manage Time Efficiently

On the off chance that an organization doesn't have a clue what it's attempting to accomplish, pioneers won't realize where to focus their endeavors. At the point when a field-tested strategy isn't set up, an organization frequently sits around idly on errands that carry next to zero increased the value of the reality. Planning enables a business to figure out which obligations are most significant, so appropriate time can be distributed to finishing them.

Allocate Resources

Representatives can just deal with such a large number of ventures one after another. Having an arrangement to control the course of the organization enables chiefs to pick assignments for representatives to chip away at that bode well to meet the destinations of the business. At the point when everybody cooperates on ventures that can have the most effect, it places the organization in a superior situation to make progress.

Prepare for Uncertainty

At the point when an organization has an arrangement set up, the executives is better-prepared to deal with vulnerability. Plans can be made to deal with conceivable future situations, so the organization is set up for any circumstance with a rundown of assets. Vague conditions can cut an organization down, yet legitimate planning can be the way to staying above water during harsh times.

Grow Existing Business

Legitimate Planning enables the executives to extend the business. At the point when an arrangement is set up, the executives can survey the qualities and shortcomings of the organization effectively. This enables pioneers to outline regions into which the business could effectively extend. Having a vital arrangement makes it simpler to recognize open doors for new business.

Chapter 3
Tools And Techniques To Improve Your Time planning

If you do a job, you need to make sure you do it right once, otherwise you just need the time to replicate it. Regardless of how busy you are, there is never a justification for your best.

Time is a fixed asset and you can't change it regardless of what you do. It only takes 52 weeks a year, seven days a week, 24 hours a day and 60 minutes an hour. You can't do anything to change that.

Nonetheless, many people have a list of things they like to do with time almost infinite. Therefore, you probably won't be able to do whatever you want.

So you must make sure that you make good use of your time. You need to increase your performance to achieve better results in your limited time. Nonetheless, you can't skimp and work quickly, because in the end, if you do shoddy work, you can pay for it. For your success, good time management is vital. You can accomplish any goals that you wish to set using an effective time planner and master list.

Many people fight for time planning, while others are efficiency champions. In reality, you need to learn how to do this, regardless of the situation. The Internet is filled with tips, tricks and processes. Yet they can't work always. The experts in time management must find those proven and utilized. The time may be difficult. Time can be tricky. And so you must learn how to blend in your day-to-day job and hobbies.

Nobody has the power to slow down time, believe it or not. But you know how to handle your time properly. Most of us want to be more efficient. Just think you'd spend less time to do the stuff you don't like and more to make you happy, happy and beneficial. In fact, some people are very efficient. You control every manageable moment so you have more time to do what you do.

It's all in the mix

It's a combination of techniques and instruments which are proven to improve your performance.... and therefore recover a large part of what is lost, and valuable, time.

Realistic tips, tools and abilities to enhance time management are given here. The dedication to change begins with time management. It's easy to manage time while you're committed. You will learn and improve your own time management by enhancing scheduling, prioritization, coordination, environmental control, comprehension, and recognizing what your behaviors, habits, and attitudes are going to change.

Planning and then preserving the expected time are the key to successful time management. Those who say they have no time don't prepare or don't conserve the time. You will have time if you plan and when to do, and then adhere to it. This indicates that your climate is programmed and restructured. Times management involves the diplomatic management of expectations of others for people who have demands made on them by others, especially other teams, managers, customers, etc. Time management is mainly about the climate, not the manipulation of your environment. You effectively allow these time management demands to occur when you embrace and acknowledge without question the interruptions and expectations of others. The pacing of the business and of the entire economy has tremendous consequences.

Training

To start with, this one principle could change your ability to deal with your time more than everything else could, which is the reason it's first. On the If you are a captive to your email framework, and especially if your pc is set up to inform you promptly upon the receipt of any approaching email, at that point I ask you to make this basic change -

it will drastically improve your command over your time. Mood killer the spring up or clamor, which informs you that you have mail. For some individuals this single greatest deterrent to fruitful time management. Set up another propensity for browsing your email at specific times in the day, when it is reasonable for you and the business to do as such - state, first when you land at your work area or start work, second just before lunch, third around an hour prior to typical business closes. You should choose when to take a gander at your messages - this control ought not rest with everybody out there who sends messages to you (nor for sure should this control rest with the spamming and infection spreading network). On the if your association has an approach, which demands that you be always hindered by your approaching messages, take a stab at recommending that the strategy is looked into - automatic email warning is the single greatest time management depreciator on the planet today.

Be set up to roll out intense changes. Be innovative to discover and present various methods for getting things done. Challenge and scrutinize your own propensities, schedules, and the manner in which you shield your time when others attempt to manage how you should utilize it. The Pareto Standard (80:20 Principle) is a straightforward simple beginning stage for evaluating where you as of now direct your time, and for distinguishing where your time could more readily be coordinated.

Really, consider how you right now invest your time. If you don't know keep a period log for a day or two. You can see and download an available time log record instrument at the business balls free online assets segment. Record all that you accomplish for a day or two, better still on the if you have shifted days; keep the time-log for seven days. You'll be astonished; for example, to what extent by and large would you say you are ready to work between every interference? Numerous directors battle to accomplish more than five or six minutes. In the event that that is you, you have to make changes.

Challenge whatever could be sitting around idly wasting your time and exertion, especially constant task, gatherings, and reports where duty is acquired or passed on from above. Don't simply expect that since 'we've constantly done it along these lines' that it's as yet suitable or even required by any stretch of the imagination. Consider why you are getting things done, and whether there is a superior way. You can see and download a leisure time the board evaluation device at the free online assets area, which will support you or someone else to unbiasedly pass judgment on your time management, and basic issues. This instrument is likewise a fantastic arrangement for time the board preparing or training.

Survey your exercises as far as your present moment and long haul goals, and organize your exercises in like manner. Particularly, plan arrangement and inventive intuition time in your journal for the long haul occupations, since they need it. On the if you don't anticipate the readiness you'll never do it, and all the work will get left to the latest possible time (sounds natural?). The momentary pressing task will consistently go through the entirety of your time except if you intend to spend it generally.

Use a journal, and an action planner to plan when to get things done, distribute or show it, and attempt to adhere to it.

In the event that you are liable to request and demand by others in your organization, and need to recondition their desires as to your accessibility and their case on your time, you should deliver a week after week plan, demonstrating your arranged exercises and schedule openings for everything that you do. This is an imperative apparatus in helping you to disclose and legitimize to others why you should organize and plan requests from others when it suits you, not others.

Weekly Activity Schedule

The things here are instances of different exercises. You can show exact timings on the if you wish. It's not important to know precisely what will fill each availability, particularly on the If you are dependent upon unusual requests, as a great many people seem to be; the significant thing is to plan an opportunity to manage what emerges, and exercises that you can foresee should be done at specific occasions. You'll realize what game of time you requirement for these unanticipated exercises, so plan vacancies to oblige them. Plan schedule vacancies to browse messages and post, yet not to manage every one completely there and afterward - edgy crises are once in a while conveyed by email or post - for the most part they'd be by telephone, so consider the originators sensible desires. Most messages you'll require just to recognize and give a sign of when you will react in full, which can be planned later, when it suits you, contingent upon the degree of significance and earnestness. Plan schedule openings for returning and making telephone calls - don't simply do them when you feel like it or when you happen to recollect. Plan and timetable things reasonably and legitimately - attempt to kill a few winged animals with one stone. Consider how best to utilize lunchtimes - and don't work through each one - you have to loosen up and enjoy a reprieve once in a while. When you've created your first week after week action plan it's anything but difficult to prop it up; a considerable lot of the spaces will rehash. You'll additionally see month to month themes as well. The more senior your job, the further ahead you have to design.

Planner

Use a simple weekly planner to oversee and ensure your arranged activities. You'll deal with your time by dealing with your activities - that implies ensuring the schedule openings you plan for your assignments. Time the board is essentially reliant on arranging exercises into schedule openings and afterward shielding the exercises from interferences, regardless of whether from other individuals or your very own interruptions.

Attempt to plan and protect time openings for everything that you do. Make records and work to them. You are at your most effective the day preceding you start your yearly leave. On the if you truly need to you can be this efficient consistently. You should likewise design availabilities for spontaneous exercises - you may not know precisely what you'll have to do, yet in the event that you plan an opportunity to do it, at that point significant things won't get pushed off the beaten path when the interest emerges.

Utilize the test: is this earnest or significant? Work might be frightfully significant, however may not require doing now. Land the truly critical positions off the beaten path first, and don't enable yourself to be diverted by the greater employments that you can do later.

The accompanying framework apparatus will assist you with dealing with your time as per critical/significant assignment reaction, organizing and arranging.

Matrix

The judgment concerning whether activities are critical, significant, both or nor, is pivotal for good time management. Most unpracticed individuals, and individuals who are bad at time the board, or in dealing with their condition, will in general invest the greater part of their time in boxes 1 and 3. Poor time supervisors will in general organize task (and in this manner their time), as per who yelled last and most intense (strikingly, din regularly associates to status, which demoralizes the vast majority from addressing and testing the genuine significance and earnestness of errands got from supervisors and ranking directors). Any extra time is ordinarily spent in box 4, which involves just capricious and non-profitable exercises. A great many people invest minimal time of all in box 2, which is the most basic zone for progress, improvement, and proactive self-assurance.

When you're looked with a heap of activities, experience them rapidly and make a rundown of what requirements doing and when. After this, handle each bit of paper just once. Don't under any conditions get a vocation, do a touch of it, and afterward set it back on the heap. Try not to begin bunches of occupations simultaneously.

27

Be totally firm in managing time assigned for gatherings, desk work, phone, and guests. At the point when you keep your time log, you will perceive how a lot of time is squandered. Take control. In the event that you keep a week by week action plan, you will have the option to control the time dispensed for your assignments.

Survey your workplace, format, IT hardware, and so on, and set it up for proficiency. Clean up your workspace and keep all administrative work recorded except if you're taking a shot at it. Keep a perfect work area and efficient frameworks, yet don't be over the top, or go through all week modifying the settings of your screen-saver.

In the event that you have one, give 25% of your duty to your successor. Delegate however much errand as could reasonably be expected to other people. On the if you can't stop interferences, at that point go somewhere else when you need time alone. Battle for your entitlement to work continuous when you have to.

Review all the normal reports you compose and get for convenience, and make or suggest changes. Set up a worthy layout for the normal week by week or month to month reports you compose, so you just need to space in the refreshed figures and account, each time. Why re-imagine the wheel?

In the event that you can, get a decent collaborator, secretary, or Individual help.

Hone up your basic leadership. In the event that you can't choose, at that point choose how to, (for example counsel, get more data, delegate, and so forth), yet don't simply give it a chance to stay there.

Figure out how to state 'No', politely, and helpfully. Try not to make a bar for your own back. Be cautious about tolerating sideways assignment by your companions to you. On the If you think that its hard to state 'No' you'll see it simpler by utilizing business motivations to legitimize your position, e.g., "I comprehend this is critical for you, however I have different needs which I should manage first to benefit

28

the business - I'd preferably concur a practical cutoff time with you over one which I can't meet." And show individuals your calendar, which legitimizes and demonstrates how you organize and deal with your time.

Continuously test cutoff times to set up the genuine circumstance - individuals requesting that you accomplish things will frequently say 'now' when 'later today' would be consummately adequate. Bid to the next individual's own feeling of time management: it's unimaginable for anybody to work superbly without the chance to design and organize.

Never attempt to eat an elephant across the board go, (for example separate exceptionally enormous assignments into absorbable lumps). Use venture the board strategies for enormous occupations.

Most importantly, pick in any event three of the above tips - ideally more - and put them into impact.

Training

Here are some ideas for time management training.

Concentrate on the reasonable issues. Time the board trainings can benefits you from a down to earth approach. Time the board hypothesis is hard to place into impact since issues are frequently brought about by propensity and condition, so preparing should focus on helping individuals to execute essential changes to their daily schedule, arranging, and particularly their reaction to other people. Effective time the board, particularly for forefront or inside administrations staff, is about re-molding the earth, as much as making changes to individual arranging and errand finishing.

use the time management techniques, formats and models here, and investigate how best to adjust them for your own kin's best advantage.

Work with the agents to recognize issues, arrangements and afterward concur promise to making changes, which should be bolstered by line directors. Catch up with balanced tutoring and training (and including chiefs to get their help).

Especially great upgrades to time the board can be accomplished with little gatherings from a similar office (max 4 preparing delegates) - including associates from a similar work group. Little bunch sizes and short sessions, as long as two hours each, empower a solid down to earth focus and results-based approach. Fortnightly sessions empower development and recognizable proof of next activities and changes.

It requires a long time to change time the board - on-going follow-up is basic or it remains hypothesis. Agents are helped by bunch discourse about time the board issues, causes, and individual challenges in actualizing change and control, which likewise enables the mentor to distinguish and mentor arrangements. Recognize down to earth enhancements and afterward formalize responsibilities to make changes (no compelling reason to do it at the same time - distinguish arrangements individually; look for upgrades in stages instead of take a stab at one major win or bust change).

Take a gander at the rudiments like journals, divider planner s, a spot to do enormous assignments free from interferences (e.g. home), better control and utilization of frameworks: cell phones, email, Viewpoint, and so on - they would all be able to undermine time-management in the event that they become experts not techniques; day-books and refreshing day by day needs records, arranging schedule vacancies (for tasks and routine exercises) and keeping the availabilities ensured. Use stream outlines to set up and plan schedule openings for routine task.

Association of partners in the gathering is basic on the grounds that common employment covering empowers schedule vacancies to be secured, and interferences to be diminished. Include representatives' directors in changes - it's to their greatest advantage to comprehend and bolster (supervisors are regularly the fundamental driver of time management issues since they don't regard their staff's time-arranging and ensured openings for ventures or huge assignment exercises). Time management requires re-molding the earth instead of enabling the earth to condition the specialist.

Time the board preparing works when individuals can analyze and create answers for their down to earth issues - distinguish issues, create arrangements, concur promise to change, and orchestrate support (common inside group, and from directors).

Most effective and proven time planning techniques.

1. Plan your day in advance

Arranging is the main, the best, and generally demonstrated ever management procedures. Right off the bat, since it serves to appropriately arrange your work. Also, in light of the fact that it gives you a nitty gritty knowledge into every one of the things you have to do. On the if you can design your every day, week by week, or month to month task, the rest comes effectively.

There are numerous approaches to design and sort out your work:

- fancy calendars and personal planner s,
- apps and tools, for example, Nozbe, Evernote, Todoist, etc.,
- to-do-lists,
- Post-it-notes and notepads.

2. E-mails

Checking and noting messages is a troublesome assignment. No one prefers it, yet everyone does it. Measurements state, "The normal specialist goes through around 30 hours seven days browsing email."

Point of confinement the time you spend on messages to the base to keep those 30 hours for work. In the event that you check it in the first part of the day, answer just to those generally significant, which need a prompt answer. Leave the rest for breaks between task or experience them toward the day's end. Additionally, make a point to check those irrelevant messages as "spam" so they don't dump your inbox.

3. Find your productivity zone

A few people are timely risers, though others are night owls. We are altogether unique and like to work in various pieces of the day... or night.

Get up too early in case you're generally beneficial toward the beginning of the day. Or on the other hand keep awake until late around evening time on the if you want to work in the murkiness. In any case, don't drive yourself to change your propensities since it is said that we arrive at profitability at specific hours. Whatever works for certain individuals, may not work for you.

4. Eat the frog

Mark Twain stated, "If you must eat a frog, it's ideal to accomplish it before anything else. Also, if you must eat two frogs, it's ideal to eat the greatest one first."

It's tied in with organizing. Do the most significant tasks before anything else, and when you're set, change to those less relevant. It will assist you with bettering sort out work process and you will get proficient.

5. Take regular breaks

Working in a persistent procedure may bring you more damage than anything else. We need breaks so our mind can invigorate and afterward refocus on work.

You can utilize the pomodoro system, or take a short walk. Peruse a part of your preferred book or make some espresso. Take breaks to expand your time the board methods and feel invigorated. This will give you a noteworthy profitability support.

6. Say "no" and delegate

Everyone has their cutoff points. We essentially can't do everything individuals need us to. It will prompt burnout and work tension. That is the reason it's so essential to be emphatic and state "no" when individuals need to dole out you extra assignments.

Keep in mind, there is nothing amiss with declining to accomplish things you're not ready to do. Just as with appointing errands. Particularly if there is somebody, who can take the necessary steps superior to anything you can.

7. Focus and block distractions

Warnings spring up messages, messages, and partners always conversing with you. Everything pulls your consideration away from work. There are numerous approaches to remain focused. You can take care of your telephone, turn off web-based social networking warnings, or square diverting sites. In any case, the most ideal path is to focus and do what you need to do. It's value to restrict your quality in internet based life to the base since it requires some investment and doesn't bring a lot of significant worth into your life.

8. Goals

Set your goals and you'll know exactly where you go. Goals are part of the organizational cycle, but in time management they are extremely important. Objectives set the way to success. We are at the top of the rung. Objectives identify key goals, objectives and vision of your company.

9. Stop multitasking

I always see job offers as one of the candidate's main skills. But throwing such an offer right into the bins is better. The fact is, our brain is weakened by numerous attempts. There seems to be a great time management approach to juggle multiple tasks one at a time. This decreases efficiency significantly.

10. Allocate your time

Would you know how long you are spending on specific tasks? Goodbye! You are likely among most people who don't know what their job is in working hours.

You will better plan a working day and workflow if you know how much time you spend on assignments, projects and various activities. The easiest way to do this is by using technology for time tracking. It will help you forecast and spend your time accurately on potential predictions.

11. Create a morning routine

When you wake up, what's your first thing? You're on the right path if it's making a bed. But you do it wrong when you test social media.

The remainder of the day will certainly be improved by your own morning routine. It is the first thing you do in the morning that will decide the day's results. Try to make a bed, then have a good breast

12. Exercise

Workouts are a great way to increase the level of time. It is a way of getting rid of pressure tension. It can also help clean up the mind of unwanted and disturbing thoughts.

Pull on and walk on your running shoes! You'll see how much routine exercise can help master the strategies of time management.

13. Tools, tools, tools

tools are an inseparable element of our work in today's highly developed world. You should apply the following to your daily work if you want to use time management techniques in full:

- **Time tracking software** – helps you to track time of your work and keep a hand on all projects and numbers.
- **to-do-list** – enable you to schedule and plan your work week;

- **Project management software** – many time tracking tools have the feature of project management. Use it to better manage your projects and clients;
- **communication tools** – Skype, Slack, Zoom, etc. – these are crucial for internal and external transfer of communication;
- **Apps helpful in creating habits** – it can be a simple calendar. The app helps you achieve your goals and it motivates in a fun way!

14. Reward yourself

Have you completed this mission or project? Well, take a break now and do yourself something. Drink a cup of tea, listen or call your buddy to your favorite music.

The tiny rewards inspire you to a great way. This reminds a little of a rabbit chasing the nose-bonded carrot. It may seem very strange, but after you have completed your task, you will find that it is worth it if you think about your happiness and joy.

15. Communicate

Proper communication can save your time a great deal. You won't understand their duties if you're not conveying your plans, goals or expectations clearly. And this will lead to conflict and incomprehension.

Often, do not forget to use special tools and applications to can your contact with your team or customers. The transmission of messages is easy, fast and comfortable.

What Time Management Techniques Do You Use?

Are you managing your time correctly? Or perhaps you are still fighting with leniency, laziness or lack of motivation? Take advantage of the above step by step and you will see how your life can better change. But remember to keep track of your time!

Chapter 4
Things Efficient People Do

It's more time that everybody needs. One way to add minutes or hours to your day is productivity. Most of them want to be more effective. Only imagine, you'd have less time to do what you do not want and more to do with the things that make you happy. In reality, some people are highly effective. You handle every convenient moment, so you have more time to do the things you enjoy.

Check out some techniques efficient people use to gain freedom.

1. Stop Multitasking

Some individuals trick themselves into intuition they are great at performing multiple tasks. In reality not very many can unequivocally concentrate on more than 1 or two task, especially on the off chance that they require focus and profundity. They trick themselves into accepting they are by and large increasingly done when in actuality, they are achieving less and the nature of the work is poor. Effective individuals realize that concentrated exertion with scarcely any interruptions prompts better work item in quicker times. Something else, the work may not be acceptable, which means burning through considerably additional time and vitality returning to fix the errors.

2. Delegate

When people take up more than they can achieve, so much productivity is lost. Don't be inspired by CEOs and executives who waste and burn the oil of midnight. Effective people may delegate tasks to others that perform them better. You can pick the tasks that suits you best and pull them through in record time without interruption, when you know how to split a mission and inspire others to contribute effort.

3. Use Appropriate Communication

Poor communication is a monstrous exercise in time wasting. A short email with poor headings or an offensive conduct might add a few hours to a task. The presentation experts take somewhat longer to consider their contact from the start. When you decide to jump on your portable, you discover your objectives. We utilize the definite language required to accomplish the ideal impact to demonstrate their messages. Toward the beginning it requires some investment, yet can shave an undertaking days.

4. Apply Structure to the Schedule

You would think that more people would feel like they have a handle on their schedule with all the available planning and development resources. Nevertheless, people often feel like their schedule is pushing them instead. Efficiency fanatics build regular procedures to maintain a disciplined approach and be able to prepare themselves for major events. The more you monitor the schedule, the simpler the unexpected can be made.

5. Give Everything a Proper Place

It takes a lot of time to pursue lost items. Hunting keys, styles and clothes can trigger confusion and frustration, especially when it's important or necessary to do something. People get coordinated very quickly. Set up a home for all your things. LEAN factories build common homes for the necessary instruments for the company. The same thing you can do. Organize clothing, paper and electronics to find what you are searching for quickly. It may take you some extra minutes to put away things, but you will save a great deal of time and frustration from finding what is necessary.

6. Time Activities

Do you truly know what amount of time you invest productively versus what amount of energy you waste? I frequently realize that I am chatting on the telephone with somebody who pays attention to productivity since they reveal to me when the call is practically finished. Effective individuals set a period for every one of their undertakings and work to keep the timetable. Give logging your time a shot discussions and exercises for seven days. At that point spend the following week setting explicit occasions for comparative exercises and work to lessen the occasions with comparative yield. You'll be charmingly amazed at the additions.

7 Commit to Downtime

Tired people do not perform well and overworked. Individuals will sacrifice their own downtime, assuming that others will gain, but in reality, efficiency is impaired. Efficient people ensure that they have rest and recovery so that they can achieve their peak. Because one excellent employee can do three average employees ' work, they are best suited to let the group relax and be highly successful.

8. Plan Projects

Effort is frequently wasted when individuals don't have a make way to progress. Eagerness is the immediate foe of effectiveness. Effective individuals realize they should set aside the effort to research and separate an undertaking into essential strides so as to make progress reliably. Truly, arranging takes a brief period. Be that as it may, thinking about the difficulties, procedure and obligations ahead of time will make for clear heading with the group. With great correspondence everybody can move unquestionably and effectively to accomplish every one of the goals in record time.

Chapter 5
Manipulate Time With Adequate Planning

We all have a day of 24 hours. However, for what reason do a few people seem, by all accounts, to be ready to capitalize on each moment of the day? We have no capacity to hinder time, amazingly. However, they can deal with their time accurately.

Have you at any point been on an incredibly tight cutoff time venture?

Temper were hopeless, supports were disappointed, and colleagues worked strange hours. Openings are as well, since someone has thought little of the measure of work required to finish the errand.

The time required for executing ventures is regularly thought little of, particularly when the work should have been done isn't well-known.

Example, eccentric events or high need work cannot be considered and the full extent of the venture cannot be permitted. Plainly this can have an increasingly adverse impact.

In this way, if your undertaking is to be effective, it is critical to gauge time precisely. In this article we take a gander at a time-expending framework and talk about a portion of the systems for evaluating that you can utilize.

Why Estimate Time Accurately?

Precise measurement of time is a key skill in the management of proj ects. Without it, you won't know how long the project will take, and t he people whoneed to sign up can not commit you to it. Most significantly, sponsors also determine whether a project has bee n successful or unsuccessful according to its time and budget. You m ust be able tonegotiate realistic budgets and reasonable time limits, in order to succeed as a project manager.

How to Estimate Time Accurately

Use these steps to make accurate time estimates:

Step 1: Understand What's Required

Begin by defining all the work required for the design. Using methods like Business Analysis, Job Breakdown Structures, Gap Analysis and Drill-Down to help explain this.

In this sense, ensure that you allow time for meetings, documents, correspondence, experiments and other tasks essential to the success of the project.

Step 2: Order These Activities

Now list all your activities in the order in which they must take place. You don't have to add how long you think activities will take at this stage. However, any important deadlines may be noted. For example, before you start work on "Year End," you might need to get work done by the Finance Department.

Step 3: Decide Whom You Need to Involve

You may make your own calculations and brainstorm them together or ask others to contribute. Wherever you can, you can get assistance from the people who do the job, because they already have previous experience. You will also become more mindful of the times you come up with by including them and will work harder to meet them. It is a good time to check your conclusions with others if you include others.

Step 4: Make Your Estimates

You are able to estimate now. We have listed a number of methods below to help you achieve this. Whatever approaches you choose, take into account these fundamental rules:

To begin with, estimate the time necessary for each task instead of for the entire project.

- Documentation rate depends on circumstances. The degree of documentation. Of example, of future project stages, you may only need a rough schedule of estimates, but you may need accurate estimates for the next step.
- List all applicable assumptions, exclusions and limitations and mention all the source of information on which you depend. This will assist you in reviewing your predictions and allow you to identify areas of risk if circumstances change.
- Assume that only 80% of the time can your assets be successful. Create time to cope with unexpected events like illness, supply problems, breakdown of machinery, injuries and emergencies, problem solving and meetings.
- If some people work on your project only in part-time, note that they may lose time as they switch between their different roles.
- Note that people are often too pessimistic about the time it will take them to complete tasks and can be greatly underestimated.

Tip:

You have decided to challenge the most accurate evaluations. This allows you to identify biases and perceptions which are not true. You may ask leaders of groups, other administrators or peers to make the estimation of time challenging.

Methods for Estimating Time

We are now going to look at various approaches you can use to estimate time.

- **Bottom-Up Estimating**

The down-to-earth calculation helps you to calculate the whole task. To measure from the bottom upward, break down big tasks into specific tasks and then determine how long each task will take.

Because each task is considered gradually, you can possibly calculate more accurately the time required for each task. The overall time needed to complete the project can then be summarized.

Tip 1:

This depends upon the case how much information you get into. The more detailed you enter, however, the more precise you will be. When you do not know how far you can go, consider dividing the work into pieces, for example, one person can finish in half a day. This is definitely a little circular, but it provides you with an idea of how much information you need.

Tip 2:

Sure, a lot of work is required, but it will pay off later on in the project. Make sure you spend plenty of time in the development phase of the project.

- **Top-Down Estimating**

You first develop an outline of the planned timetable using past projects and past experience as a guide to top-down evaluation. To ensure accuracy, it is often helpful to compare top-down estimates with the bottom-up estimates.

Note:

Do not presume that the lowest estimates are inaccurate if they differ significantly from the lowest ones. However, the opposite is more likely to occur.

Use the top-down estimates instead to question the validity and adjust the bottom-up estimates accordingly.

- **Comparative Estimating**

You look at the time it took you to perform similar activities in other projects in comparative estimation

- **Parametric Estimating**

Using this method, you calculate the time needed for one deliverable and multiply it by the necessary number of deliverables.

For example, if you need to create pages for a website, you can calculate how long it takes to make one page and then subtract the total number of pages to be created each time.

- **Three-Point Estimating**

So add a pad of uncertainty, three predictions can be made—one for the best case, one for the worst and one for the most likely case.

While this strategy involves a further effort to produce three different figures, this helps you to create more reasonable expectations based on a more realistic assessment of performance.

Tip:

Perhaps you do not know who does every project in the early stages of project planning—this may impact the amount of time it takes to do the job. The experienced programmer, for instance, should be much more swift than somebody with less experience while designing a computer module.

This can be incorporated into your calculations by good, worst and most probable predictions that provide the basis for each view.

Preparing Your Schedule

You should plan your project schedule once you have determined the required time for each mission. Attach your estimates to the draft list of activities you generated in the next phase. A Gantt charts can then be created to plan and allocate resources for your project and to finalize milestones and deadlines.

Tip:

If your project is complex, it might be helpful to define your plan's critical path. This helps you to emphasize the tasks which cannot be delayed if your deadline is reached.

Key Points

If you want to execute your plan on time and on budget, you have to calculate time accurately. Without this ability, you will not know the length of your project and you will not be able to get the people you need to help you achieve your goals.

However, with the stress and pain associated with it and loss of credibility, you run the danger of committing to unrealistic short deadlines.

To estimate time effectively, follow this four-step process:

1. Understand what is required.
2. Prioritize activities and tasks.
3. Decide whom you need to involve.
4. Do your estimates.

Use a variety of estimating methods to get the most accurate time estimates.

So how do you Prioritize Work when everything is in number 1

Understanding the goals of your job affects your project's progress, your team's dedication and your leadership role. Clear goals are required for all projects— especially large, complex projects. Most quickly, you can rely on technological tasks to include changing orders, reprioritization and frequent surprises, no matter how well prepared. It's only the order of things in natural order.

To project managers and leaders one of the greatest challenges is the exact focus of the day-to-day work. You can enter information on the device even if you have the best project management software on the planet. Therefore, for all the other pike ventures you do not want to fall to the position of weeping' top priority.'

Just as you must be vigilant and have the right type of project, wisdom is needed to ensure that nobody works on the goals yesterday. To get this right requires a lot of training.

Here are a few measures to prioritize tasks which have a lot of moving parts to help you manage your team workload and meet time limits.

1. Collect a list of all your tasks.

Pull all you could possibly think of in a day together. Do not worry about the number of items or the order in front of you.

2. Identify urgent situation versus important situation.

The next move is to see if you need immediate attention to activities. It is a task that will have serious negative consequences if not completed by the end of the day or in the coming hours (missed consumer deadline; missed publishing and release deadlines, etc.). Check if you are now completing a piece of work, if there is a high priority requirement.

3. Assess value.

Then take a look at your important work and see what your business and organization holds the highest quality. As a general practice, you want to correctly identify what activities are of high priority over the others.

Of e.g., prior to internal work, concentrate on client projects; software setup for the new CEO before server re-configuration; answers before writing training materials to the support tickets, etc. Another way to evaluate the quality is to see how many people the job impacts. For particular, the higher the stakes are the more participants or factors.

4. Order tasks by estimated effort.

If you have tasks with priorities, check their estimates and start with whatever tasks you think you will do the hardest. Productivity experts recommend the first way to start the longer mission. Nevertheless, if you find that before you finish the shorter job, you cannot focus on the meatiers, then go with your intestine and do that. Until you dive into deeper waters, you can take a small job away from the list.

5. Be flexible and adaptable.

There is uncertainty and transition. Remember, and often when you least expect them, that your priorities change. You also want to concentrate on the things you are dedicated to completing, though – and here's the trick.

6. Know when to cut.

You may not be able to get to all on your list. After prioritizing your tasks and reviewing your forecasts, delete the remaining tasks and concentrate on the goals that you know you must and will achieve during the day. Then take a breath, immerse yourself and get ready for anything.

Chapter 6
Organize Your Life And Find More Time

All seem to report that they are now distracted. No wonder, given the wealth of knowledge, events and opportunities we have at our disposal only a few decades ago, this means that one of our most valuable resources — time — is becoming more difficult to control.

That said, many people accomplish incredible things in the same 24 hours that we all have available every day. So what do many people know they don't know?

What's Really Important to You?

We have distractions surrounded us which steal our time if we aren't careful. Everyone is busy 24 hours a day, but it's important that we all do different things. The problem is whether your life is full of endless time zombies or whether you are involved in doing things that are important to you.

How to Organize Your Life to Maximize Your Productivity

Here's a simple exercise to look at where your time is going on an average day and to help **prioritize the important stuff**:

1. Take out a piece of paper and divide it into 3 sections
2. In the first section write "Sleep – 8 hours" or whatever that number is for you
3. In the second write "Work – 8 hours"
4. Now in the final box write down the following things and the time they take
    1. Things that you *have* to do (showering, commuting, eating, etc.)
    2. Things that you *want* to do (activities, time with family, etc.)
    3. Other things that you currently do (TV, Facebook, etc.)

4. Anything else that takes your time each day and isn't captured already

Now you just wonder if you are happy with your time in that additional 8 hours. If you wish you could spend more time in your hobby or family, but you could find that every night you spend some hours before TV, maybe you want to change this.

Eliminating Huge Time Sucks from Your Life

There are also aspects of our lives that you may need to do right now, but the time is not always the best. You might spend one or two hours commuting from and to work, for instance. Every day of your life, that is the time you lose and never recover.

Other issues could include getting children off and picking up when you can take turns with other families. Maybe you're hopping on Facebook, or on TV, and before you know it, it is time for the bed. Limitation can reveal a lot of waste productive time in those places.

Using "Dead Time" Productively

You will want to figure out the most productive way to do this if you still need to drive around or do other things. For example, during your shift to up-train in some regions you might start listening to personal development or business audios. You can listen to audio every week for 5-10 hours by transforming your car into a driving school... 250-500 hours a year!

You may include your children or just have them sit at the kitchen counter while cooking or cleaning, so that you can talk. In that way, every evening, when you cook and eat dinner, you have a nice time with the children. Ultimately you are asking how you can optimize the time spent in the things "must do."

It's Your Time… So Organize Your Life to Get What YOU Want

It is up to us to make the most of all, we all have a limited amount of time each day. You change your life drastically by understanding what is important to you and making the most of your dead time. Remember it's about your perfect life – not someone else – so focus on what works for you.

Chapter 7
Creating A Learning Plan

No one has ever written a plan to be broken, overweight, lazy or stupid. That's what happens if you have no strategy. Let us take a few practical steps to handle your own professional development.

I am sharing a strong example of a personal development plan with you, but first of all I would like you to fully realize why a personal development plan is relevant.

Why Do You Need a Personal Development Plan?

Have you ever been on holiday with little or no planning?

I did and I was disappointed not only because I had to schedule everything on this adventure, but rather because of the exciting and spontaneous journey.

When you always have to think about where to stay, what to eat and where to go it is very difficult to enjoy the trip absolutely. You can fly much more quickly if you have at least a great pictorial view and an idea of where you want to go and a simple plan of what you want to do. If you have a more detailed plan, it is even simpler.

The way of life is the same. Most people just live with little or no thought, so it is no surprise that they are frustrated or wonder "How did I come to this place?" This is why planning a plan in advance is critical.

It fascinates me that most people are better off scheduling their holiday than they are planning. Maybe because it's easier to escape than adjust. You could end up feeling furious, depressed and not happy with your life if you do not think or plan in advance.

The personal development program has other benefits.

You can only look into your project, and remember where you want to go, if you ever feel lost in life. Your guideline for life is a personal development program! You will become more aware of your potential and take better decisions in the process by "developing." your future.

Most people undergo research, because they don't understand the areas of personal development that can lead to mastery in any field. Hard work can't be replaced. You can see the personal development and progress of your career when you set a goal, make a plan and work on it every day. Except the boundaries you set with your thought, there are no limits. Engage in lifelong learning. There is always something to know, although you're at the top of your profession. If you live a purpose and growth-oriented life, you will become invincible and see the entire future open before you.

You should know where you go and how you are going to go if you are a driver, and wish to make your journey more pleasurable. Good preparation reduces the risk that something will go wrong. The same goes for a personal development program—it increases the chances that your life moves in the right direction.

You probably ask yourself, if you like the idea of having a personal growth plan: "Where to commence?"

So, Where to Start?

You can organize your thought through a personal development plan. We prepare and think constantly in our minds but often miss important detail and do not build a realistic plan. This is why a lot of' plans' stay in our minds alone.

A personal development plan is a system that determines what is important for you, what you want to accomplish, and the abilities that you have to achieve and improve over time.

Normally, it's not done immediately if you create or model something new. This is why you must be prepared to take time to implement any significant project. It is great to have a personal development plan model in order to make things simpler.

Personal Development Plan Template

Personal development plan will help you form your thinking and build a tactical plan to achieve your objectives. You can take time to make a detailed plan, if you want to do something important. In designing a personal development plan, there are some important things to consider. Here are measures to build a good personal development plan:

1. Define your goals
2. Prioritize
3. Set a deadline
4. Understand your strengths
5. Recognize opportunities and threats
6. Develop new skills
7. Take action
8. Get support
9. Measure progress

1. Define Your Goals

What are you worried about? What are your new abilities? What would make you happier? What achievements? Have you any visions that you are going to fulfill? Would you like to move on to your next career stage? Would you like a better job?

The first step is to identify your very important objectives. It can contribute to your work, but also enhance or boost your personal life (such as losing weight, starting a new hobby or learning a new language).

Step 1: Write down 5-10 goals, which are important for you to achieve.

2. Prioritize

Of all the objectives you have mentioned, which one you find to be the most relevant. This is your main objective that will depend on you. You may want to change your career or you want to get a good physical form or new skills.

Is there any transferable skills that are necessary for your success (skills that you can transfer to various areas of your life? When you develop your speaking skills, for instance, you will achieve greater trust, better relations with others and even business success (e.g. more successful negotiations and more sales). The purpose of a personal development plan is to assist you in improving your knowledge, developing new skills and enhancing important life areas.

Step 2: Take a good look at your list and select one goal, which is most important to you to work on first.

3. Set a Deadline

If you've got a goal, but don't know when you want it, it probably won't be happening. However, if you plan to carry out a major project in a very short time, it will probably not happen again. If you are preparing, you must be practical, realistic and timely. It's better to plan this year to triple your income than to think "One day I want to be a millionaire."

How long will it take you to achieve your goal?

Once a reasonable timeline has been developed for your target, you need to commit to doing it. Be serious about it. Be careful about it. Neither will anybody else if you don't take your plan seriously.

Rather than focusing on problems and barriers, think about how great you'll feel when you're done. It's also possible to determine how you reward yourself to achieve your goal.

Step 3: Set a deadline.

4. Understand Your Strengths

Everyone in the world has something good and in some particular areas has more than average ability/strength. You can still be a good parent, a good listener or a caring person, even if you're not a talented singer, actor or artist.

What are your key strengths?

Ask your friends and family if you are not sure about the answer. Tell them, "What do you think my greatest strengths are?" Perhaps your answers will surprise you. What makes you unique and special is your key strengths. Nobody can ever take you that. It is very important to be aware of your strengths for your trust. Are you an organized, patient, enduring, smart, courageous, quick learner, talented and open-minded...?

Step 4: Once you understand what your strengths are, write down which of these strengths can help you to achieve your goal.

5. Recognize Opportunities and Threats

Your existing behaviors and habits can either help you to attain your goal or not. What are your habits or acts that hinder your goal?

There are things you need to stop practicing.

You need to stop fume, stop buying junk food, and stop worrying about things, etc. for example, if your goal is to live for 100 years. Write down five things you're doing you're going to stop doing.

On the other hand, some new measures will make it much easier for you to reach goals. Which acts can you choose to start to achieve your objective? You can start managing your money, start writing down your expenses, and begin to spend less, etc. if you plan to save more cash, for example. Write down five stuff you pledge to start to do.

Step 5: Create a start doing and stop doing list!

6. Develop New Skills

An individual development plan is a plan to get to the location you want to be from. You have to give something in return if you want to get it. You will have to learn new skills if, for example, you want to go into the next phase of your career.

You should learn about marketing, sales, entrepreneurship, financing, etc. if you want to start your own business.

A Quote by Brian Tracy:

You have to pay a price in full and in advance for all that you want in life. Decide what you want and then assess the price to accomplish it. Keep in mind that you have never done something before — you have to do something you never did before. You must be someone you were never before. If you want, a price calculated by: money, time, commitment and personal discipline will have to be paid. Decide what it is and start today to pay the price.

In other words, you should develop skills that you never had before and work on them as soon as possible to achieve something you have never accomplished.

Which skills or knowledge will help you to achieve your goal?

Step 6: List the skills that you need to learn to help you reach your target.

7. Take Action

If you want to accomplish a major objective, then you will have to take some steps to achieve it.

Step 7: Write down the most significant steps you will take within your set time frame, at least 3-5.

8. Get Support

Who can help you achieve your goals more quickly? Of example, you can suggest consulting with a qualified counselor if you want to change your career; you can have a fitness coach if you want to lose weight; you can talk to a financial adviser to help improve your finances.

Step 8: List anyone who you can think of who would be able to help you to achieve your goal.

9. Measure Progress

Your own success is the greatest incentive to stay successful in achieving goals. It's still something, even though it's a little improvement. It is important to recognize that you are improving and to document stuff you do well.

What can you do differently if something is not going so well? If anything doesn't go well, you need the methods you are using to adjust (or improve). You will achieve the same results by doing the same things. You need to change something if you want better results.

Step 9: Set out things you need to change and decide new strategies you are going to try. Your job is to make things work for you.

A personal development plan is a very effective way of evaluating your life, identifying what you care about, and getting involved in the most important things. We are so busy with our daily activities often in our lives that we rarely have time to reflect or prepare critically.

Concentrating on your own personal development program strengthens your strengths and makes your hopes and desires a reality. Your ability is infinite, and it is a way to harness your many strengths. your personal growth.

Setting goals and expectations for what you are trying to achieve will boost your personal development, whether on a short or long term basis. Self-confidence is the critical factor in all that you do because you will do almost anything with the appropriate amount.

Personal Development Categories

Concentrating on a number of categories of personal development, such as personal skill, development and personal strength, will create personal improvement habits. Education and skills are the foundation for personal growth. We prefer to recompense individuals above average in our culture. In particular, those who know more than the average are paid more than the average. You improve your level of competence and your ability to succeed in your profession through training and experience.

I outlined seven main personal improvement categories, which are the subject of most people:

1. Personal Skills

Were you trying to increase your job skills? The highest paying, top people in their profession are those who focus on improving their professional know-how. Those skills can be the abilities you've been trained with and skills learned deliberately. You are very helpful in your personal and business life in which areas you excellently need growth.

2. Personal Growth

Personal growth is to develop you, to get out of your comfort zone and concentrate on making yourself a better edition. Human beings and the human mind grow constantly, not stopping. Your job is to be better than you used to be yesterday.

3. Personal Power

Your connections and resources support personal power Creation of an ever-expanding communication network increases the number of doors open to you. Having people with the same ambitions and willingness to help you can have a direct impact on your performance. Money in the bank offers independence and the ability to take full advantage of certain chances.

4. Personal Improvement

The development of people comes from good working habits and a positive attitude. It is important to think about good work practices before you act. Set priorities on a list and take into account possible consequences before the end. Holding a positive mental attitude reduces the time it takes you to accomplish your goal.

5. Personal Empowerment

Encouragement of a positive image and imagination in your everyday life will speed up your goals and improve your individual potential. Thinking innovation means always finding simple, good, more convenient and cheaper ways to accomplish the job.

6. Personal Analysis

It is very important to be aware of places where you are naturally talented and to research areas where change is needed. The first step forward is to be honest about where you are. You should continually assess where your objectives and aspirations are concerned.

7. Personal Objectives

Ambition is lost if no clear objectives are in sight. A pivotal step is the creation of short and long-term goals. A plan will help you understand clearly that methods are required to reach your desired destination.

Aspects of Personal Development

There are several facets of the disciplines of personal development that make success possible when you practice them properly. Some of these areas include – setting goals, preparing and arranging events and reflecting on your important tasks.

Personal Development Examples

Goal Setting

The setting of the goals that take only a few minutes in the early morning of your day. It can be as easy as buying a spiral notebook and writing your 10 goals every day. This programs them into your subconscious mind profoundly.

Planning Your Day

At the end of the day preparing and organizing can help you prepare better for the next day.

You can start visualizing your important tasks when you schedule your day and put it on paper to make sure that you focus on completing them all day long.

Concentrating On Your High-Value Activities

Focusing on your tasks of high value should contribute as much to your performance as any other discipline. Promoting the things with the highest value would make a significant impact on your achievement.

Importance of Personal Development

What you're doing most of the time is what you're doing. Knowledge, thoughts, experiences, all sums up and feeds into your brain.

From the wake to the end of the day when you close your eyes. Everything you experience is a variable, but some things are more important than others.

Personal Development Goals

Developing personal development goals for work can make the difference between success and failure. Some personal development goals for work examples include the Golden Hour and the 21-Day Mental Diet.

Personal Development Goals for Work

The Golden Hour Rule guides your day's course. You will make a huge difference in your emotions from the beginning of your day and by spending your first hour into yourself and start seeing positive results in your day. You'll start to get a better idea of yourself and start to improve your personal development.

Personal Development Goals for Work Examples

The 21-day Mental Diet ensures that you wake up early and invest in yourself for at least the first two days. With this additional time, you can define clear objectives to be met at work. This can help you achieve a benefit and increasing your productivity and efficiency. Training can also be a motivation for you. To benefit more, you must know. Try to read something informative, motivational or motivating every day before you go to work.

Personal Development Goals for Employees

Personal development goals are very important to workers because without an intent or vision, the emphasis is not on what is most important. Selecting areas of focus, set planning and progress reporting are some of the main personal development goals for employees for example.

Leadership goals are identical, but you identify development needs, training opportunities and then devise an action plan.

List your findings and assess areas in which more structure is required.

Personal Development Skills and Objectives

Personal development goals are ongoing personal development, improved prospects and the use of potential opportunities. Through setting time to the important people in your life, conducting action activities that motivate you to do at the highest levels and researching growth efficiency, you will continue to climb the ladder of success.

Personal Development Plan

Having a personal development plan allows you to gain a better understanding of your life and prepares you better for anything that happens in your life.

What is a Personal Development Plan?

A personal development plan is your roadmap to your life and your future success. You will think "what is a personal development plan."

Why Do You Need a Personal Development Plan?

The reason you need a personal development plan is because having a plan would help you to assess and remember where you want to go.

Effective preparedness increases the likelihood of success and reduces the risk that something will go wrong.

How to Write a Personal Development Plan

Once you write a personal development plan, you know what you want to do, how you need to change and evolve and a schedule which will prepare you for the most important tasks for the next day.

Personal Development Cycle

A personal development process is an ongoing period consisting of curiosity, knowledge and reality in three main components. In a continuous loop each element appears first.

We continue to become part of our routine and lose our childhood interest as we mature. You should never be so obedient that to learn and improve, you lose your appetite.

Not always bliss is ignorance. Awareness of our old and bad habits is the only way to make positive changes. To enhance your knowledge and understanding of our strengths and weaknesses, you have to develop a sense of personal awareness. After your reality. Upload. The world is yours, but first of all there is a need for self-growth.

You will draw on strengths and work constantly to strengthen areas of weakness by understanding and recognizing what your strengths and weaknesses are.

Personal Development Planning Checklist

The easiest way to monitor yourself and to ensure that you are on track to meet your end goals is to build a personal development planning checklist. Start with as much detail as possible by writing your objectives. Write down your weaknesses and strengths. First, write down a list of tools you have available to help you establish yourself.

Courses and seminars, books, blogs or networks are included. Do not be afraid to request help from others. You can interact by visiting family and friends or even by joining a group dedicated to the fields you wish to concentrate. The best way to gain invaluable experience and life skills is to learn from a mentor.

Personal Development Plan Guide

Every daunting job must be personal growth. Through this guide, you will discover vital ways to get better without concern or pressure.

You should, however, do some self-reflecting and answer questions about personal goals before setting up a plan.

Before implementing a specific action plan, you must ask several questions:

- What do I want to make out of my life?
- What are my goals and ambitions?
- What is currently standing in my way of achieving these goals?

You may create a personal plan that includes a few key elements after answering those questions. The main components you must focus on are a particular goal, towards which you constantly function, prepare and pave a path, be mindful of the challenges and realize the greater motivation of your activities.

Personal Development Plan for Work

You must concentrate on SMART goals while designing a personal work development plan. SMART stands for' Simple," Measurable, Achievable," Relevant,' and' Time-Bound.' You will boost personal and professional lives after an easy-to-remember acronym. You need to report a clear action plan in order to make progress that you can see and track.

Several examples of personal development strategies provide answers to the following questions:

- What do I want to learn?
- What do I have to do?
- What support and resources will I need?
- How will I measure success?

Be as specific as possible with your answers. The more precise, the more the progress can be tracked. When you see how far you have come and how hard work pays off, you will gain confidence and feel fulfilled.

It is also important to focus outside the workplace on certain personal goals. Compared to the work plan, you have to focus on key issues to achieve your goals in the Personal Plan.

Here's an example of a personal development plan:

- What are the important goals that you want to achieve?
- When is your set deadline?
- What are your biggest strengths?
- Who or what biggest threats?

Personal Development Plan Template

For order to reach your objectives, it is important to have a detailed plan.

I have developed a model to promote your ambitions for a personal development project.

The blueprint includes six key measures to assist you in taking action and evaluating your progress.

Phase 1: List the top ten goals that you want to accomplish. Please note that

Step 2: Write down which of these ten is your main concern and why.

Step 3: Set a certain timetable for your target.

Phase 4: Write down your weaknesses and strengths.

Concentrate on three of each and then explain how your strengths can be useful to achieve this goal.

Step 5: Write down actions to achieve your goal. Step 5: These can be stuff to add to your everyday routine or things to get rid of.

It helps you reach every goal more quickly.

Step 6: This step marks the progress you are making. Write down what you did well, what you did, what you still had to learn and what you learned knowledge or skills.

Chapter 8

How To Build An Action Plan To Meet Your Home Business Objectives?

The SMART goals are known by most people. The challenge is to develop and execute a plan to achieve these goals. In the first days of the goal, optimism motivates people to achieve success, but it is not long until life as usual and the goal is a far-flung memory. Research shows that less than 10% of people feel their goals are being met. 90%, which is an incredible number, does not.

The question is, what do the 10% do not do the 90%? There are many variables that decide whether or not objectives are accomplished, but 1) a strategy and 2) the dedication to the project are two important components.

Here's how to build a strategy if you're prepared to achieve your goals.

1. Make Sure Your Goals Are SMART

SMART goals give you direction and a time limit to reach them. SMART goals are: Specific: The goal is clearly defined. "There is more money I want to make," is unclear. Specifically, "I want to make $10,000 a month."

Measurable: The goal must be quantified so that you know that it has been accomplished. That's where it helps in general. What's more in additional money? A certain number of dollars can be calculated.

Achievable: it is good to set goals that stretch and challenge yourself but if your aim is not achievable, you will be disappointed and ineffective.

Relevant: Your priorities must fit into your ultimate life plans.

Time: You set a date for achieving your goal.

Please note that targets work for big milestones such as $50,000 a year to work, as well as smaller projects such as a 30-day business website, or five individual customers in two weeks.

2. Work Backwards to Set Milestones

One obstacle to meet the goals is the fact that it is always too long before the deadline and too late for most people to take action. Installing mini-goals that drive you towards the main target instead of taking a look at the amount of time you have and your goal.

For example, if it's your goal to make $10,000 a month in your business within six months, create mini-goals of how much you'll earn at the end of one month (i.e. $2,000/mo.) and three months (i.e. $5,000 per month). If a third month arrives and you hit or missed your mini-goal, you will know you're on the track and off.

3. Determine What Needs to Happen to Reach Your Goals

During this stage, decide what is needed to achieve your small and large goals in time. You want to attract more clients or buyers using the $10,000 a month goal example to make more money. In this phase, you want to know how many customers you have to pay for your company for $5.000 and $10.000 per month. How many outlooks will your marketing funnel have? How many slots do I have to generate for sales?

4. Decide What Actions Are Required to Reach Your Goals

Which activities and goals do you have to do daily to reach #3? Of example, if you have to negotiate two sales with 10 people, what actions do you have to take to find 10 people? Which acts are you going to take to follow the 100 leads to find 10 individuals to talk to?

For industry, advertising is the standard in this section; it also involves delivering a good product or service and ensuring that consumers and clients are satisfied, so that they will return and/or refer to new prospects.

5. Put Your Actions into a Schedule

You should have a list of tasks when completing #4 to achieve your goal. Now is the time for a routine schedule to include these activities. These are activities that you undertake every day to create resources and direction. You are also responsible for building and delivering the product or service.

It can be a struggle to add more activities to your daily routine when you begin a part-time business in an already busy life, but to achieve your objectives is important. One way to do it all is to know how your time can be handled and maximized.

6. Follow Through

Once the above steps have been completed, you will need to set your daily schedule and objectives during the work on your project. Meeting your plan is the next step. Do the everyday tasks that you have delegated to do. Find a way to keep yourself focused if you think things aren't going well. It sounds like a joke, but most people do not accomplish their goals, because they don't do the job regularly and consistently. The strategy does not work in most situations, people simply leave.

Keep track of your successes and progress while you are there. Specify the time every month to review how well the plan works and change it if you don't make the progress you need. The true test of whether or not your home business succeeds is not simply that you have a good scheme, but that you have a strategy. Most businessmen would like to think that they have a strategy, but then abandon it. The solution is to look forward to the targets, to invest in ways to celebrate small milestones and to always keep an eye on the prize.

Chapter 9
Best Tools And Techniques In Organizing Your Time

Effective time management starts by demonstrating just how much time you actually spend on your projects and assignments, and then by evaluating how you can better manage them.

People frequently ask, "Where to begin planning time?" One of the best places to start is to ensure that you have the right tools to produce. The right tools, after all, simplify every mission. So you always want to use the right tools whether it's a domestic development plan or a work that can be done. The same applies to planning.

One of the first things you should do for beginners in time management and for those who want to boost their performance is to determine the resources you use, because if you do not have the right tools it will be difficult for you to control your time.

The management of time really takes place in these crucial areas: activities, resources, people and data. To this end, everybody must have important tools at their disposal.

The Essential Time planning Tools You Need are:

1. Commotion list – a strong commotion list is the cornerstone of any productivity process. It is the one you need if you only have one time management tool. You're your best friend and should always be with you.
2. Calendar – It can be hard to manage your time when you understand how it is spent and where it is spent. To track, schedule and organize your time, a good calendar is important. The time for your plans and activities, not only meetings.
3. Address Book–Most people are underestimating the power of a good address book in our over-connected social world. When you

need to communicate with this important touch, LinkedIn or Instagram will not help. Collect all address information you get. Treat mobile and e-mail numbers as silver.

4. Notebook—A decent notebook is the most often lacking resource in the time management process of people. Probably, on your desk, you may have a pad or a bunch of post-it. You need a spot, however, where you keep all your notes. And one place to go and see if a piece of information is necessary.

The Right Tools for Productivity

At least one of these resources is lacking for people who are not able to manage their time. Make sure each of the simple time management tools are usable. Never matter if your phones are paper-based or app-based, as long as it is available and used.

For order to manage time better, everybody needs resources. It is important to have calendars, address books and notebooks. I think it's a big mistake that people ignore the ability to imagine the job. It's not so hard to manage time as I felt before. To keep your job organized, you can use paper bits. Effective time management includes numerous sections and different approaches. Regardless of whether you are employed, at home or at school, planning our time is often important to our successful lives.

To carry on your career, deliver your projects effectively and to receive promotions or pay increases, you should learn to focus on activities that contribute the most to your projects and clients. Check these Critical Time Management skills and strategy. The more emphasis you are on, the more you will achieve and the more possible it is for you to leave your office on time. You can not only achieve better results at work through active time management skills, but also avoid stress and lead a more satisfying life outside of work.

In less time, the following methods will allow you to achieve the right things.

1. Start your day with a clear focus.

The first goal of your day should be to figure out what you want to do that day and what you need to accomplish. While reading your inbox and answering questions and addressing questions, make sure you understand this. It might take as little as five minutes to set the clear focus for your day but it can save you time and effort for several hours.

2. Have a dynamic task list.

Collect and regularly update the tasks and the things you must do in a list. Review this list often and add new things as they appear. Ensure that your list offers a quick summary of all issues that are urgently and relevant, including tactical, relationship-building and organizational activities.

3. Focus on high-value activities.

Once you start something new, decide how your plan, your team and your client would be better impacted if you had to deal with this right now. Resist the tentation of firstly clearing small, insignificant objects. Start with the most important things.

- To help you assess which activities to focus on first, ask the following:
- What does my client or my team need most from me right now?
- What will cause the most trouble if it doesn't get done?
- What is the biggest contribution I can make right now?
- Which strategic tasks do I need to deal with today to help us work smarter tomorrow?

4. Minimize interruptions.

The more you focus on important tasks throughout the day, the more productive you will be. Identify and find solutions to events that are likely to interrupt your job. Basically, not interfering is one of the most critical time management skills. For example, do not monitor emails or answer your phone if you are in the middle of an important thing. It can be hard to recover it once you have interrupted your flow. Instead, focus on a project alone until it is done. Control yourself.

5. Stop procrastinating.

You can benefit from an internal commitment to (deadline), if you have difficulty staying concentrated or continuing to procrastinate. For example, schedule a meeting within two days where you present your work and when your activities must be done. It's also very effective early in the day to do the most difficult tasks and give yourself small rewards as soon as you have finished them.

6. Limit multi-tasking.

Many of us do multi-tasks and feel that when we do so, we can't focus adequately on more than one thing. To avoid multi-tasking, follow these tips: plan your day for meetings, return appeals and do detailed work on your desk in blocks and set specific time to meetings. Whenever you are busy, stop and sit for a minute, quietly.

7. Review your day.

Pass 5-10 minutes before you leave the office to update your task list every day. If you have done what you wanted, give yourself a punch on the shoulder. When you think the effort of your day was short, decide what you will do tomorrow, to accomplish what you need. Leave the office to pick up the thread on the next day in high spirits.

Make a concerted effort of these vital time management skills and you will find your days and tasks running far smoother!

Some necessary time planning tools to look out for

Every tool has realistic features to help manage and optimize time in every business or personal situation.

Create a Plan

1. Week Plan

You can quickly see what's on your plate throughout the week with Week Plan. The application has functions and goals pages, and a parking lot for items that are later to be submitted. To add a new job, select any day of the week to make it as important or pressing as needed.

Although Week Plan gives you a good picture of the upcoming week, it also provides a monthly plan to help with longer durations. You can try out the platform for free with three schemes or look at paid-in packages with additional features including subtasks, review and the integration of Google Calendars.

2. Weekis

Weekis is the one for you if you prefer easy, quick weekly schedulers. This no-frills alternative is a web-based app that allows you to enter your tasks on a daily basis. It also makes planning one day at a time simple.

Weekis allows you to look at the week, to reorganize drag-and-drop activities, and to save your posts, if you create an account free of charge.

Use an Organizer and Calendar

3. Trello

Trello is a robust tool for managing any size task. The software includes tables, lists and cards for coordinating tasks using the Kanban process. They can coordinate and build checks and deadlines of projects. You can also collaborate with staff.

Apart from the wonderful manner in which you and your team can coordinate, Trello provides a useful calendar power-up. Click the Display menu from the top right corner to add this option to one of your panels, choose Power-Ups, and then select allow next to the calendar. Next to the top board menu a reference to the Calendar option will appear.

As a paid option, Trello is available free of charge with Trello Gold, which offers features such as large attachment uploads and saved searches. The mobile Trello apps can also be viewed or links listed below.

Download — Android, iOS

GQueues

GQueues is another important organizational and timetable management application. Include repeated tasks, subtasks, communication and sharing, assignments and comments, labels and prioritization with the look and feel of Gmail.

Fundamental features of the software including private and paid plan options are available for free. Note that compatibility with Google Calendar is a part of the payment plan— although the GQueues Lite (free) contains the calendar gadget. For mobile devices, GQueues is also available.

This is a convenient option if you use a host of Google services like Google Drive, Google Contacts, Google Calendar and Gmail.

Download — Android, iOS

Keep Track of Your Time

5. Toggl

Toggl is a vibrant monitoring tool that includes the development of projects, customer and team management, multiple workplaces and reporting tools. Tap Timer, enter a name for the task and press Play button to start tracking an event. Tags for quick organizing can also be included.

73

Toggl provides integration in the Basecamp, Asana and GitHub software. You can monitor your time and access your things from anywhere with access via the web and mobile apps.

You can register and start using Toggl with all its features free of charge. Payment plans include other options, including planning, time reviews, and the inclusion of team members.

Download — Android [Broken Link Removed]

6. RescueTime

RescueTime can be a good option if you prefer the desktop application to record time. The Windows, Mac, and Linux systems and Android can be downloaded. Once mounted, choose and pick the days and times you want to monitor the most successful and distracting activities. The software then records your time automatically.

You should never think about failing to start the clock for an event with automatic time tracking. RescueTime provides ways to set goals and show a preview every day. You can also review performance, priorities and task efficiency reports.

With its limited features RescueTime Lite is free to access and RescueTime Premium is a premium plan despite additional features including regular goal updates, full report history and disabling the website to help reduce interruption.

Download — Android, Linux, Mac, Windows

Prioritize To-Dos

7. Doris

Doris is a very quick way to give priority to your task list. You can add various chaos to your list, edit it and include annotations in this document. Select one and drag it to the position in the list to assign the tasks.

You may also show your current day, week, month and week or month task history. When every to-do is completed, you will see that options for removing or restoring it are open. Doris is a basic web resource, free of charge.

8. Todoist

Todoist is one of the most common apps for task lists that can help you organize and keep your to-dos up. The software provides color-coded levels of priority, so that you always know the key. Recurrent dates, sub projects and tasks and convenient reminders can also be created.

The transfer of tasks is another dimension of time management that Todoist can assist with. You can share the workload with an easy-to-use platform through collaborative tools, project assignments and opportunities for discussion.

Todoist is available on the Web and on mobile devices free of charge and open. Additional features include Gmail and Outlook browser enlargement and integration. Additional features for paid plans include location-based alerts, file backups, project templates and Team Management.

Download — Android, iOS

Delegate Tasks

9. MeisterTask

MeisterTask is a visual resource very useful for project, task and team management. Set up various sections for different projects or sub-projects and each requires assigned tasks. The software includes due dates, notes, labels, alerts, appendices and lists of controls, all enabling delegation. MeisterTask helps you to print or export data for team time monitoring.

A short summary of your activities can be found on the main screen. Including Slack, Zendesk, GitHub, Zapier, Dropbox and other integrations with MeisterTask.

MeisterTask includes a free and restricted edition and a paid scheme that allows unlimited integration, seamless workflow and custom backgrounds. Apps for mobile and desktop computers can be accessed via the Internet or applications.

Download — iOS, Windows or Mac

SHOULD YOU Use a tool to manage time? You have a great chance of benefiting from dedicated time management technology if you juggling with words, resources and deliverables continuously..

Chapter 10
Time Planning Apps

Nobody can deny the numerous advantages of engineering. It has definitely allowed us, above and beyond what once was expected, to interact, perform and develop our resources. You definitely miss a trick if you don't take advantage of one of the hundreds of time management apps and software available. But how do you learn what software to use with so many phones? Okay, this will depend on your needs, but we have built a list of 18 of the best time management apps to help you tackle the most popular challenges.

Take a look at the list, find yours and increasing your productivity Find yours and improve your everyday productivity

1. Scoro

Scoro offers the tools you need, including time tracking, accounting, reporting, project and task management for an effective time management approach.

Top features:

- Track both actual and billable time and transfer the hours to an invoice
- Automate late invoice reminders, scheduled and recurring invoicing
- Email invoices to clients based on the hours worked
- Extensive project, task, and client management
- Reporting on work, sales performance, budgets, etc.

Scoro integrates time tracking with project management and CRM, strengthens teamwork and allows all your business processes to be managed in one location. What is so fascinating about this method.

2. Asana

Asana incorporates project management, processing and coordination components and assists in team-wide management of projects without e-mail.

Top features:

- Break your work down into tasks, and assign it to team members
- Organize your tasks into projects for roadmaps and timelines
- Review milestones, and check on your team's progress
- Get notified about projects updates
- Use project dashboards to get a quick overview

The thing about this tool is so special: Asana is a very simple tool with a simple interface. Check that if you're a small team of tasks that are not too complicated.

3. Trello

Trello is known for visualizing projects on a cardboard screen, which manage fast and quick daily tasks.

Top features:

- Simple task management on a cardboard
- Creating unlimited task lists
- Image and file sharing
- Organizing lists by dates or priority
- Commenting and collaboration

What's so unique about this tool: Trello is the most visual way for teams to work together on any project, from startups to Fortune 500.

4. Clarizen

The technology for project management built on Clarizen's cloud has one objective: to help the company move forward.

Top features:

- Unlimited number of projects
- Automated and repeatable processes, alerts and workflows
- Social collaboration
- Budget tracking and expense management

What makes this tool so special: Clarizen provides configurable workflows – adapt Clarizen to the way your business works, not the other way around.

5. Toggl

Toggl is a time monitoring application without hate that combines with decades of different project management systems. It is the perfect complement to your existing tools to make you more successful all day long.

Top features:

- Unlimited projects and sub-projects for accurate time tracking
- Reports featuring team progress
- Online & offline time tracking

This software is so interesting: Toggl is seamlessly integrated with your favorite tools for the efficiency of Trello, Scoro and Asana.

6. Replicon

Replicon is a robust multifunctional platform that helps businesses monitor the amount of work expended and compensate to their customers for completed projects.

Top features:

- Time tracking and time sheets
- Multiple billing rates for different users
- Project budgeting and expense management

- Analytics on time usage

Which makes this software really interesting? Replicon calls on large companies to more effectively control their resources. The tool provides an overview of every minute you work.

7. Timecamp

Timecamp uses time monitoring at the end of the month for billing buyers, calculating task productivity and paying staff.

Top features:

- Automatic billable & non-billable time tracking
- Integrated payment getaway
- Budgeting in $ or time
- Powerful reporting
- Mobile & desktop apps
- **What is so interesting about this tool:** Timecamp makes it easy to measure wages on the basis of the time spent, besides accounting customers.

8. Bill4Time

Bill4Time is a very comprehensive cloud-based time billing software. It simplifies your billing; helps you recover lost revenue, and let you track time and expenses from anywhere.

Top features:

- Track billable and non-billable time
- Get daily, weekly and monthly work summaries
- Client portal
- Invoicing and online payment options
- Extensive reporting on accounting, projects, etc.

What is so interesting about this tool: Bill4time provides a wide variety of information on the performance and earnings of the team, and much more.

9. Nutcache

Nutcache is an all-in - one device that offers time tracking and invoicing. It is intended for small teams which project-based account their customers and schedule their time more effectively.

Top features:

- Time tracking and billing
- Expense management
- Linking projects and finished tasks to clients

What is so interesting about this tool: Nutcache has a user-friendly interface, suitable for teamwork.

10. Hubstaff

Hubstaff helps to monitor the work time and the leisure time of your team. This is an excellent option for companies who try to control the work time (not just the time they spend on employee).

Top features:

- Tracking the time spent on tasks with screenshots
- Billing clients for projects
- Reporting on the team's time usage
- Emailing custom reports to clients
- Making payments to employees based on the time worked

What is so interesting about this tool: In addition to the time spent on various websites and desktop applications, Hubstaff also monitors the time spent.

11. Freckle

The goal of Freckle is to make time tracking fast, simple and almost enjoyable for your team.

Top features:

- Time tracking
- Invoicing and billing for the time worked
- Dashboard that shows your time expenditure
- Categorizing people and running reports
- Mac timer app, iPhone app, mobile web app

What is so interesting about this tool: Freckle uses tags to track and navigate projects between checkable and non-checkable tasks. This makes it easy and fast to insert time entries.

12. Teamwork Projects

Teamwork lets you calculate your time and then record your actual time against it. you think you will need to complete tasks. You will soon become very specific in your predictions, and know exactly how long it takes for certain tasks to be completed!

Top features:

- Estimating and tracking time spent on a project
- Sending invoices based on the time worked
- Custom time reports with export options
- Tracking time on the go

What is so interesting about this tool: The invoicing features for collaboration are not as good as other applications but combine them with all your favorite accounting apps such as QuickBooks, Harvest, Xero and other.

13. Bric

Bric is an analytics-built time billing technology. They offer input into the future, designing plans, scheduling jobs and tracking how people spend their time.

Top features:

- Configurable time tracking
- User roles & rates
- Utilization reports

What is so interesting about this tool: Bric has a number of project planning and management capabilities in addition to robust time-billing.

14. Harvest

Harvest is one of the most popular devices on the market for billing. Harvest makes it super easy to track and recharge your customers accordingly thanks to its simple interface and light feature set.

Top features:

- Creating estimates and invoices based on the time worked
- Time tracking from any browser, Mac, iPhone, or Android
- Integrations for tracking time across all your favorite project management tools
- Real-time reports on time spent

What is so interesting about this tool: Harvest is focused on doing one thing and doing it well.

15. Avaza

Avaza time tracker allows you to start a timer on your phone, stop it on your tablet or any other device and track time spent on a given job.

Top features:

- Time tracking on the go

- Time entries on invoices
- Timesheet approvals
- Expense tracking

What is so interesting about this tool: Avaza provides a range of scheduling and project management features in addition to time tracking and billing.

16. Active Collab

Active Collab incorporates time and project management to promote the scheduling and recording of creative projects. In addition, this platform offers group coordination and networking capabilities in real time.

Top features:

- Creating tasks with multiple users and deadlines
- Filtering tasks by users, dates, and labels
- Commenting on tasks and mentioning colleagues
- Gantt-like timeline for planning
- A shared team calendar for collaboration
- Time tracking and sending invoices

What is so interesting about this tool: Active Collab improves the team's collaboration and makes it more fun. Every user can set a custom theme for their platform for quick personalization.

17. ClickTime

ClickTime allows companies to monitor both time reviewed and time used by workers. The project budgets will be managed completely and accurate time sheets will be provided.

Top features:

- Online timesheets and billable time entries
- Time tracking with stopwatch

- Dynamic billing rates
- Analyzing project profit, costs, and billings
- Reporting on employee and project performance
- Forecasting the time needed for tasks

What is so interesting about this tool: ClickTime gives you more insight into your use of your time than other methods to pay for resources. This concentrates on enhancing the performance of your team and helps you manage your budget and resources more effectively.

Chapter 11
Why Do I Waste My Time?

As a coach for time planning, people always come to me when they are overwhelmed, depressed and feel like they don't achieve the things they most want to do in their lives. You're still trapped. You're at a point you don't know what to do.

One of the first things that I do first is to recognize the time-wasters, the obstacles that stop them from going forward and doing what they want.

I assume we all engage in activities that do not make us happy or productive from time to time. I certainly did, but once I became a businessman and realized how important every second of the day, I made the necessary adjustments— that there really wasn't any time to waste on things that didn't grow me or my company.

We all want to succeed in life, but sometimes we waste our time doing things that prevent us from reaching our full potential. And often, until somebody points them out, we don't remember such things.

We have to look for ways to operate more smartly in order to eliminate time-wasters, so we spend hours by hour. To begin with, eight things are here that good and efficient people never waste time doing (and you shouldn't):

1. Productive, successful people don't get sucked into social media.

Being on social media—checking notifications Facebook, scrolling through pictures on Instagram, reading quick updates on Twitter, *whatever*—it's part of everyday life. But if you don't control how much time you spend on it, the hours will fly by and you won't have accomplished anything on your to-do list.

So either put a time limit on it—set an alarm for when you need to minimize it, close the app, *do something else*—or only get on *after* completing necessary work projects. Use social media as a reward.

2. Productive, successful people don't go through the day without a plan.

Successful people have the goal to fulfill an overall plan, a laser-focused scheme. I know I write things down, but that's not a long list of things, just the two or three top priorities I need to achieve that day.

Specify your top priorities and split those big tasks into more reasonable steps and you'll find that you want to do them and get them off the list.

3. Productive, successful people don't do emotionally draining activities.

You have to focus on things that drive your life positively, if you want to venture into a genuinely prosperous world. Productive people don't waste time on things that exhaust them emotionally.

Make confident that your operation will make a positive impact on your life before you engage in activities on your calendar. Then think about saying no to it if you assume it isn't. Often, do not feel compelled to give you a correct response at the moment something is needed. Think, think, and know that it is all right to say no to your time requests.

4. Productive, successful people don't worry about things they can't control.

Successful people realize you don't really have any worry, particularly when you can't do anything about a situation.

5. Productive, successful people don't hang out with negative people.

The average person you spend most time on is said to be five people. So you have to surround yourself with the best people if you want to be the best.

Make sure you remove harmful, toxic power. You have to uncharged what's weighing you if you want to soar in life.

6. Productive, successful people don't dwell on past mistakes.

Good people are making mistakes. All of us make errors. It is not the same mistake to learn and to evolve from mistakes, and to become a better person because of them that is the secret to succeeding.

Therefore, if you make a mistake, come to know that the failure is made and that you cannot return to the past. Concentrate on what you know and build a plan to move forward positively.

7. Productive, successful people don't focus on what other people are doing.

It's nice to be motivated by what other successful people do, but it is time to change the attitude if you compete continuously with the next one and bring it down.

Be motivated by others, but focus your thoughts only on yourself, which is the leading man.

8. Productive, successful people don't put themselves last in priority.

We all go through periods we can't sleep or practice enough, because we have a major project to work on. But you must place yourself first in the priority list of long-term success and happiness.

Some great ways to do this is to end your day with something you love to do—perhaps it completes a great practice, meditates, reports and reads your favorite book. Do what works for you. Do what does.

Because you'll feel happy, centered, and powerful all day long when you start your day by doing something you enjoy and which is good for you.

Are there stuff that were time-wasters for you on this list? Replace them so that you can step into your best life.

Super-Fulfilled People Never Waste Time on These 9 Things

Sometimes it seems that we're wasting most of our time chasing stuff that we think is going to get us feeling better only to find that we wasted the time with insignificant things that did nothing for us.

All these are shades of the same thing: anxiety, remorse, perfectionism. We are what happens when we live, we don't think we have enough, that we aren't enough.

But the really experienced person works on an entirely different level. These dark forces that keep so many of us behind, they have no mind. We have a clear mind, an open mind, and a fascinated eye that keeps them focused on what is most important and free their time from the precious moments we need.

That person is, of course, a sign rather than a real person. Something or someone they're striving to. We all need to work on things, but we can continually arrive at a position of success and begin to realize these values within our own lives by fostering appreciation and pursuing our muse.

Do not waste your time on what is not important. What is not important. Don't get suddenly pulled down. Go on: don't linger on the past. Be a great person; be religious generous; be the person you would admire. – Allegra Huston

I always focus on this great achievement every day, but it is a success deserving of all.

What does this fantastic man look like? You may be simpler than what you do to describe by what you don't do.

Such nine things are never lost by super-fulfilled men.

1. The cult of busyness

We must first understand how to find meaning in order to fulfill ourselves. And that really means we know what the cultivation of occupation really is: feeding constructive signals to the brain by preserving perpetual motion, to confuse us if we don't do what we should actually do.

Super satisfied people know the occupation is not equal to purpose or quality. We seek to achieve its purpose and to develop meaningful interactions rather than doing things that take away when they are frustrated that they don't do what they need to do.

2. Pursuing other's definition of success

Super satisfied people realize that happiness and value are achieved if they know themselves and do not follow the definition of success in society.

Instead of making their own way based on a keen understanding of their own interests and longings, the many people in the world do what they do because of societal pressure and refuse to drink Kool aid.

3. Regretting the past

Through default, one does not need to regret the past to be fulfilled. Those who have been achieved exclusively are not generally perfectly satisfied with their experience, but have learned and continue to do so today.

Nobody told me when I was younger what it meant to work hard. I just heard how a true hard-working mentality felt like before I got older and I'm thankful for this discovery.

For a while, though, this lesson made me look back with disappointment at my years and prospects. But now, after years of hard work I'm more pleased with my efforts than ever before in my life, and the past won't weigh on me as it used to be.

Today, even if you are not perfectly happy, your actions will help you to remember and end regretting the past.

4. Small distractions that keep you from what is most important

Distractions abound now more than ever. We can access catalogs of distractions from smartphones and tablets of any kind: social media, sports, endless news to chat websites and any poison you need.

It is unbelievably easy to rationalize these distractions all day and persuade yourself that they take very little time or are successful ("for example, they minimize my stress").

But all these little distractions contribute to your precious resource over time, time.

The person you are will meet the person you could have been on your deathbed. You want to die because you have waste hundreds of hours on publications or on pointless games? The super-fulfilled person knows the stakes and does not spend time on distractions.

5. Worrying about what others think about you

The very intention to achieve requires a complete break from other people's ideas and views. It is not possible to achieve it without doing it first.

Yet super full people know another thing: we do stuff for ourselves and generally don't concern ourselves with what others do, especially those outside our family and close groups of friends. They are worried about what others think they don't know that most people think that same thing and don't worry about what others do.

It's a pointless exercise that cares about what other people think of you, and that has been a great exercise long ago.

6. Worrying about current events

Really satisfied people realize just how great every day of life is and they don't allow it to bring them down even though they know what is happening in their life and in the whole world.

Worry is nothing but positive, and people who are super happy are not stuck in the belief that the world collapses around them. I know that life feels like that sometimes, but in reality it seldom turns out so poorly and still has a positive outlook, realizing how thankful I must be.

7. Drama

Many viewers like to spend time watching pointless dramas. This is understood, embraced and kept moving by the super fulfilled man. Because they don't need it, they are beyond it. You're not trying for something outside to make them feel whole and can see straight through the average person's tiny difficulties.

8. Perfectionism

The unbelievability of those who are accomplished is in contrast to perfectionism: the belief that things are not enough. Appreciation and appreciation have mastered.

Frequently, the perfect time never arrives, the perfect conditions never come together, and never does the perfect opportunity arise. Perfection is just a front that we don't work on if we feel we're not enough. Outstanding people know it and let them not be held back by incompetence.

9. Hate

Those who frighten themselves use hate to cause this terror. Nevertheless, when someone is genuinely happy, the outside world does not bother them, since their happiness comes from within.

You know how lucky you are to live your life and thus to have empathy for others who are less fortunate than to hate to think that any person or group of people could jeopardize their role.

It's a busy day to end, so you look back and wonder "Where did you go? It's time for you to be productive now. What do you need to do? With those little distractions that take away the tasks that really matter a bit of your time was most likely consumed.

You should respect your time. It is valuable. What you spend your time has an enormous impact on your performance. Increased productivity and the maturity with which you use your time will give you more time to do something that matters to you, such as runs, hobbys or other ventures.

Making yourself successful by eliminating the biggest waste of time in your life and you might find that you have more time than you know.

1. Multitasking

Trying to do more than one thing reduces the productivity. There is no multistakeholder mind. You need to slow down when your brain transitions between tasks, so you are less busy.

You simply switch between two tasks, without concentrating really on either. The consequence is that the focus is not focused on either task, so that neither task is performed in the best way possible. You will be able to concentrate on one thing at a time—better results will be obtained with fewer errors.

2. All things email.

Mail could be one of the largest black holes in sucking space. Your focus breaks down every time you get a warning that you have a new email. Instead you answer meaningless emails or try to find the right email in a broken file.

Try to check your e-mail by fixed times, such as once a day, once a day and once a day.. Keep your email search until the most important job of the day has been accomplished. In this way, you have done what you need, even if email distracts you.

3. Social media without a purpose.

If you use the Social Media for private use, it may be a great distraction, but it can also be a time when you use it for legitimate work purposes. Social media can enable the company to boost sales and advertising when it is used effectively.

But you must know how to use it effectively, as with any other device. It is all too easy to read random papers or to be drawn into pointless "analysis." Next, you have to figure out how your company benefits most from social media and remain focused during your use.

Firstly, stop checking your behavior in social media obsessively, for company and for personal usage. Check your news feeds regularly, or see how many people follow you, your attention and your time are gone.

4. Pointless meetings.

Meetings are necessary when important decisions are to be made, but are often perceived as a waste of time because they are not used efficiently. The problem is not only that it takes time to sit and meet without any use; it also takes time to prepare for such an unsuitable meeting and to write and read e-mail messages concerning the meeting.

Unproductive meetings cost businesses about $37 billion annually, according to one estimate. So if you fall in sight at conferences, try ways to re-establish your position. Make sure the meetings are held and a moderator who concentrates on them.

5. Disorganized work environment.

Do you have sticky notes and paper scraps on your desk? Is it a chaotic mess of random files on your desktop that completely covers the background? Looks like an eruption of paper and documents in your registry office?

If so, your disorganization may well waste your time by making it difficult to find anything and making it unprofessional to boot. The workstation has to be decluttered. You will be able to get information and move on to the next things quickly if everything has a location.

6. Too much socializing.

There is a fine line between maintaining a relaxed and friendly working environment and enabling chatty colleagues to enclose you. Nothing is wrong in socializing with colleagues; nobody wants to stay quiet all day long. But when you are not patient, engaging with co-workers is easy to lose valuable time.

The use of headphones during concentration could help prevent colleagues from speaking. Don't be afraid to say to others you're busy right now and should stay focused. If you want to have lunch or hang out, you can always see, but try to protect your working time— job.

7. Refusing to seek clarification.

You are given a large mission. It's a perfect opportunity to demonstrate your talents and you are assured that you can destroy them. You dive in, but you gradually remember you are over your head and you are not sure exactly how the final product will look.

Instead of seeking clarification, however, please pick up the phone or address. You say you're going to work it out. It's a huge waste of time because you let pride get your attention. You should be successful and efficient when you have questions or are unsure how to continue with a project and get details.

8. Online distractions

Ah, the internet. Nothing is more distractive that we have at our disposal an endless source of information, entertainment and shopping and fun. You are protected from digital disruptions by a number of strategies. If you know your websites are soft, try to remove these tentations by using a website blocker.

You can start with 20 minutes and work up to 45 minutes or an hour by setting up a timer for some increments. Stay focused on work all the time and you can make a break for yourself.

But, even if you only want to use the internet for your job, it's easy to drive online research from one thing to another, so make sure you really concentrate on what data you're getting from online sources.

9. Too many breaks

The 3 pm. You hit a doldrum and are searching for a pick-up–a snack or a drink to get you through the day, maybe. The question is that you are lingering and never really concentrating.

This tiny break could become a huge waste of time. Would you like to eat your time away (or worse, smoking)?

Mindless food isn't healthy to start, especially if you don't care about what type of food you snack. Is coffee or soda too much. And your health may be affected by cigarettes. Try to go for a quick walk if you need a break to clear your head. It's safe and can improve your mindset to function.

10. Ignoring your mental exhaustion

We put in longer hours than ever and have higher rates of burnout. Ultimately, we are often too busy to focus on things properly and end up spending more time. You are more susceptible to distraction and are likely to find it hard to concentrate when you're continually tired.

You won't be successful if you're not mentally prepared to work well. Take a pleasure and prioritize rest. When you are awake and ready to take on the world, the time you spend rest will pay dividends.

11. No clear goal to motivate you

This can be the most dangerous in the long term of all the things on this list. You could end up spending your time if you don't have a large scale strategy and clear targets. You need to be focused and have a clear idea of what you want to do if you want to be successful.

It's quick to let another one-day stretch into another and never really do anything if you don't have a motivation to stay focused. That is when it is easy to give all the other tentations on this page. By chance you're not going to succeed. It needs commitment and endurance. You're just winging and wasting your time if you don't know what the game plan is.

Chapter 12
Can I Really Do Without Time Planning?

Your day is probably one of the most critical productivity habits that you can make. you probably already know. You don't know, however, how a day plan could work for you. In your life no two days are the same and what's going to come up, you never know!

Maybe you even tried in advance to schedule your day. But it just irritated you when in the first few hours your project failed. And you felt very overwhelmed while trying to stick to the program.

I'm listening to you!

Good news, however: routine scheduling takes many forms and dimensions. And I firmly believe that everybody has a great day strategy. It is just a question of finding the sort of schedule you want.

A day plan does not have to be a day routine

For example, a common misconception is that from one day to the next they have to be identical or similar. Just like a routine every day. While routines in particular definitely have benefits, they don't have to cover the whole day. For example, you can have a morning routine and every day after that something else happens.

Don't just try to create a day routine, if your days are unforeseeable or unique. It's all right to be different every day. And for each of us we can still make a terrific day schedule.

The golden rules for day planning are one day at a time, one day at a time. The night before you schedule your day, and prepare only once a day in depth. You don't even know what's going to take place tomorrow unless you schedule your days a whole week in advance.

Planning one day in advance helps you to get the most up-to-date information about the present, relevant and tomorrow's agenda (such as meetings, set commitments).

Of course, when something else comes up, you can always delete or move things around... But the problem with changing your schedule during the day is that each small adjustment feels something of a failure. And this is an open invitation to feel frustrated and defeated.

So, it's very boring to move things around a calendar, don't you think? I mean, I'm thinking, **the whole point of a plan is to have something we can follow without much thinking**. Constantly having to adjust it kind of defeats that purpose.

The flexibility attribute

How flexible is your day plan?

There is a degree of flexibility in every day program. And "calendar projects" solution is at the bottom of the versatility scale.

Even if you build in unplanned space, each job is closely tied to a timetable. And this reduces the choice you have when you decide when a flying job is a good time.

The more chaotic your days and the more frequent interruptions and activities that happen during the day, the more versatile the regular scheduling process has to be.

We have the daily commotion list. The versatile daily schedule is there.

The object of what you do (the very definition of the word ' plan') is and when you do it (today!) you have a time frame attached to it.

You can do the activities in any order and whenever something else happens you can simply include it in your list without having to change something. The everyday commotion list allows you maximum flexibility.

A commotion list for your day is a day plan. Of course, you're irritated if new tasks emerge all day, when you put so many things in your chaos list that you can only complete it all in a day. Generally speaking, more elastic is the smaller the commotion list. Hold the regular to - do list on the shorter side so that accidental tasks and interruptions are possible.

Finding your flexibility sweet spot

Adjust, adjust, and adjust

But maximum flexibility isn't always the right answer. There is a downside to too much flexibility.

A strategy will help us focus on action throughout the day and not answer concerns about what to do. Those questions we answered during preparation already! But we often have to make some decisions about the next thing to do with a flexible day schedule once again. And these actions add only to our frustration during a busy and stressful day that we are less efficient.

There are also specific benefits that come with a less flexible approach to day planning.

The more precise, for instance, the more (what and where) our purpose is to do it, the more likely we are to do this rather than wait. When we don't have a particular time on a mission, we lose some of that value.

Finally, putting tasks on a calendar makes you know the duration of each task and reduces the risk of getting too much on your plates in one day.

And if we want to have everything? Flexibility and all the advantages of a comprehensive program. Is it possible? Is it possible?

Definitely! The key is to find a candy-plate for your versatility: just enough flexibility so that you do not have to change plans throughout the day.

The way you find this sweet place is to start someplace and then make small changes to increase or decrease versatility. As you know that you need a lot of flexibility, start the daily chaos list. Then you can check with a little more structure and rigidity.

You may also use other special commotion lists strategies that provide the same advantages as "calendar jobs." Of example, each project can be assigned a time estimate to ensure that you do not plan too much for your day.

Adding more structure to your daily to-do list

Lowering flexibility

Here are a few ideas on how to add a bit more structure to your daily list.

- Only assign a specific start time to a few tasks you are likely to procrastinate. Set a reminder on your phone or computer for those tasks.
- Sort your list based on priorities and work your way down from the top. No skipping!
- Section your commotion list into large time blocks and sort your tasks roughly into these time blocks: try morning, afternoon and evening for example.
- Mark your commotion list items with priority markers (A, B, C) and add something that signals urgency (e.g.!) to any items that MUST be done today. Use these to make quicker decisions what to do next throughout your day.

You need a daily schedule with plenty of flexibility if the days are unpredictable. The most versatile kind of day schedule is a routine commotion list. But there are too many downsides to the versatility, so that you can check with the following ideas to add a little more construction to your everyday concussion list:

How to make your daily commotion list more structured

- Only add a specific start time to one or two tasks you are likely to procrastinate
- Sort your list in the order you need to do the tasks, then just start from the top
- Use priority and urgency markers to know what can wait if necessary and what can't
- Break your daily to-do list into large time segments (e.g. morning, afternoon and evening)

General Day Planning Tips

- Only plan your next day in detail to ensure you have the freshest information
- Plan your day the night before
- Add time estimates to your tasks to make sure you don't over-schedule your day.
- The more interruptions and spontaneous tasks you have throughout the day, the shorter your to-do list should be

Chapter 13
Time Management Tips To Grow Your Small Business

Time is valuable, particularly in the management of a small company. Although being your own boss is a fantasy for many, it's a big dream. Without a question, all the things in your to - do list appear never to you. It can seem like there are an endless number of tasks–from accounting, inventory, to the networking and advertising of your business.

If you want to maintain a semblance of the balance between work and life, you really have to be able to control your time. There's never more than 24 hours a day, after all. Some entrepreneurs respond with intent and intention to this fact of life. Some freak out. Others freak out.

Don't worry if you're in the latter category. You can take control of your time and make your job effective, profitable, and fairly stress free with the right time management techniques. The following management tips will help you to make sure that your work is done when in the workplace, so that you can enjoy your time away from work.

1. Set goals

The setting of goals is important for every good strategy for time management. You need to identify your priorities, in terms which are transparent and realistic, to ensure you are engaged in activities that support your business goals in the short and long term. After all, you can feel overwhelmed and unsure where to start if your aim is to "grow your business."

Several businesses have noticed that the SMART priorities approach allows them to stay on the mission and monitor in order to counter this paralysis. Wise objectives, which reflect "wise, measurable, achievable, appropriate and time-limited," include simple step-by-step activities in support of your target.

One SMART target, for instance, could be, "Increasing the traffic on my website in the next six months from 1,000 to 5,000 unique months ' visitors."

- **Specific:** The goal states exactly what needs to be attained.
- **Measurable:** The goal can be measured with a specific tool, in this case, Google Analytics.
- **Attainable:** Rather than vaguely wishing to increase visitors — or setting a goal too high to reach — this goal states a specific number that is well within the realm of possibility but still ambitious.
- **Relevant:** Instead of measuring something like site sessions or overall site visitors, the goal is to reach potential new customers — always crucial when growing a small business.
- **Time-bound:** There is a due date set at the end of six months to attain this goal.

You will work backwards to define the different steps you need to reach your SMART goals once you have set them. All else is a time-waster theoretically. Your day-to-day strategy will focus on work and work related to your business development and income generation.

2. Prioritize wisely

It will be time to plan once you have set your goals and the individual tasks that you must perform to achieve them. You want to make sure that you do things, of course, but they should be the right stuff.

First Things First's co-author Stephen Covey provides advice on how to handle the urgent commotion list. He suggests assessing what's on your plate and putting each job in one of the following buckets:

- **Important and urgent:** If a task falls into this category, you know it must be done right away. Focus your energy on completing your most important and urgent tasks before moving on to less time-sensitive items.

- **Important but not urgent:** These are tasks that may appear important, but upon closer examination, can be postponed to a later date if necessary. While these items are likely integral to smoothly run your business — perhaps you need to update your website or find a more efficient payroll solution — they are not do or die.

- **Urgent but not important:** Tasks that make the most "noise," but when accomplished, have little or no lasting value. In this category, you might find a sales call from a potential vendor seeking to work with you, or perhaps a coworker drops by your desk unexpectedly to ask a favor. Delegate these tasks if possible.

- **Not urgent and not important:** Low-priority stuff that offers the illusion of being busy. Do these later.

Write down the "important and urgent" things you have to deal with today. Check the list as you complete each one. It gives you a sense of satisfaction and can inspire you to go down the list so that less important items can be addressed in good time.

3. Just say no

You are the manager. You are the boss. Do not hesitate to do so if you have to refuse your offer to do what is truly important and urgent. The same applies to any projects or events you have identified: be prepared to take on more successful tasks. Know how to avoid waste of time later.

4. Plan ahead

Spring to workday with no clear idea what is to be done is one of the worst things that you can do. Although it may seem like time consuming to think ahead for five to ten minutes rather than just doing business, I am shocked how much more effective you can be by spending a little time preparing the rest of the day.

When you schedule your time wisely, instead of waste time springing from one thing to the next (and often losing anything) you can concentrate on one project at once. It makes it easier, not harder, to work. Consider one of the choices below in your daily routine depending on your personality:

- **Plan the night before:** At the end of the day, take 15 minutes to clear your desk and put together a list of the next day's most pressing tasks. It's a great decompression technique, and you'll feel better sitting down at a clean desk in the morning.
- **Plan first thing in the morning:** Arrive a few minutes early and assemble your prioritized commotion list (see tip two). This may prove to be the most productive part of your day.

5. Eliminate distractions

You continue to be aware that when you're in the middle of an important job someone stops you. Track self-induced interruptions, in particular social media interruptions. The mobile is very helpful, but it's also very addictive and one of people's most dangerous wasters.

It can take a big workout, but shut the door and turn your mobile off to optimize your time. Planning a break during the day to collect messages, make telephone calls, speak to employees, etc., instead of "still on"

6. Delegate more often

One of your most valuable management tools is the ability to delegate if you recruit talented and dedicated workers. A successful small company depends on the ability of the manager to see what lies ahead and not get mired in everyday business. Look for ways in which others in your group can perform those tasks. You recruited them for that, aren't they?

7. Track your time

How long are you really packing productive minutes every week? Time tracking is an extremely useful tool for calculating how long a job takes. You can quickly and easily clock in and out of different tasks or activities during the day with a simple time sheet monitor.

Change jobs or activities with only one button or directly from your computer using the TSheets mobile app or monitor time. Then deliver accurate, real-time reports to see exactly how your valuable asset is being invested and what it is lost.

8. Take time for yourself

In the heat and heat of a successful business, this tip is often overlooked. Nonetheless, it's important to take care of yourself–i.e. to get plenty of sleep and practice–to keep track of progress.

In fact, one study from Harvard showed that sleeplessness could make the average worker lose up to 11.3 days of productivity every year. In another study, regular exercise helped improve the focus, sharpen the memory.

It's vital for your mental health and can help you keep energized and excited about your job that you have some free time every single day to spend on people and things you enjoy outside of your company. After all, keeping things in perspective is crucial. You have decided to be a small business owner and you are able to wake up every day to a day full of possibilities.

Chapter 14
Cultivating Your Passion Instead
Of Following It

For our happiness, our jobs are important. Many people work for at least eight hours a day and most people continue to think of it in their time spent. So it would have been safer for us if we spent one third of our adult lives living, right?

"No life worthy of the name consists of anything more than the continual series of struggles to develop one's character through the medium of whatever one has chosen as a career."
- Juan Belmonte

The most common answer you get when asking people about their work is: "It's okay, but I don't think that I'm excited about it." Universities are filled with students who feel that there is a perfect job for them, which they enjoy. Years and workers are passing; they earn a degree and more work. But there is a space. No zeal. There is a void. Therefore, the hunt will continue, but you won't ever get your dream job. What you can bet on is that obligation will rise every year, and it will be difficult to change directions. And, when we have the freedom to check various options, we are smarter about our jobs.

There is not much doubt that most people have desires that are always there to be found. If the workplace reality doesn't suit this vision, it can often lead to chronic frustration and uncertainty.

The main point of this book is that you don't discover your dream job. What's one of my favorite quotes reminding me?

"Life isn't about finding yourself. Life is about creating you."
-George Bernard Shaw

So instead what are we going to do? Concentrate on maintaining rare and valuable talents that you cannot forget. The secret to your loved career is to acquire professional capital (skills and valuable relationships in your field) which will allow you to manage your career.

So as Charlie Munger said: *"the safest way to try and get what you want is to try and deserve what you want."*

You must first of all follow the mentality of a craftsman.

The artisan's philosophy focuses on your craft's value to the world. Contrary to the passion-consciousness, you concentrate on developing skills that are useful in the future instead of seeking a perfect job.

But it's a warning: Which particular area of practice would I choose to draw on precious and uncommon abilities of all the things I can do? There's no easy answer; most of us have lots of interest and skills to draw on. Deploy an experimental approach and start testing your choices instead of showing you what you should?

Following your passion is one of the most important pieces of career advice. Career coaches repeat it endlessly, although it can be frustrating for many of us. After all, most children who have a passion for sport and fashion design for those who enjoy this sector do not have enough jobs in sport management–and even 14 year-olds know this.

But what do those 14 years-olds, and 44 years-olds unhappy in a job, do if they don't really know what their passion for career is or how to make it a financially appropriate and exciting work?

Four recommendations for your career:

1. Realize career passion is rare

It is rare for Mr. Newport to feel passionate about a career. He cites a report by the psychologist Robert Vallerand from the University of Quebec, which found that the top five activities students enjoyed by university are: dance, hockey, snowboarding, reading and swimming. Lower than 4% of the sample did, in fact, describe some job or education passions; the remainder were hobbies. "If we don't have any specific passions to pursue, how can we follow our passions?" asks Mr. Newport.

"Telling someone to' follow their desire' is not merely an act of naive hope, it is also the foundation of a work of confusion and fear," he argues.

2. Become a craftsman

He advises you to cultivate a talent instead, in his second rule, to become a craftsman, until you are so good you can't be ignored. He compares the mentality of the producer which focuses on the quality that you create in your work with the enthusiasm which focuses on the value that the job provides you.

"The artisan's mentality is liberating: It allows you to leave your own self-centered doubts about whether your work is' just right,' but put your head down and plug your head to get really better, he argues. No one owes you a great job, you have to deserve it, and the process isn't going to be easy," Mr. Newport says.

Rare and valuable work tends to be the best. You need exceptional skills to protect it - what he calls the wealth of your career. Through constantly focusing on building your skills through conscious training, growing and continuously improving yourself, you will be so successful in achieving these jobs.

He states the consciousness of musicians, athletes and chess players. You just don't play, you hone your skills. Once this craftsman approach is established, he argues, passion will come. You should, however, make sure that you do not waste it or give it up before it flows entirely.

3. Seek the elixir of control

He states that people who love their professions want power and, this is his third principle, refuse a promotion when it leads away from what they admire and master. He calls autonomy the dream job elixir: "It enhances people's happiness, loyalty, and a sense of accomplishment, to give more control over what they do and how they do it." Firstly, you need to take more control of your working life before you develop the workplace to give your employees or customers. The second trap is that once you have the opportunity to get more leverage over your working life, your boss will resist your attempt to gain more freedom. (Example: A person who leaves the university and tries to turn to freelancing professions so soon that he is never sufficiently good to demand).

4. Develop a mission

His fourth principle is for the area right beyond the current cutting-edge to be a remarkable and highly sought-after task, once you have expertise and power, to build what he calls the "adjacent possible." He encourages you to do this by taking small steps. Only think, act large. Think small.

It is well-structured, with Mr. Newport as a guide, which takes you through his own and other career experiences, draws examples, applies them to study and threads them into all four rules. It's a good novel, giving a different inclination to the concept of passion for career.

How to Find and Make Time for Your Passion Even When You're Busy

Some of us are fortunate to take on the kind of career that encapsulates our passions, our purpose of life, our personal essence and our technical ability, and that allows us to exercise them in a 40-hour gig at the same moment.

Others are happy to work in areas where our passions may not be injected into our work but where we can use our technical skills, expand our experience and comfort in areas beyond our range... whilst also occasionally paying for our rent and buying a new handbag.

In the latter camp, I happen to fall. After my master's degree in English, I was offered a position in a prestigious energy consulting firm during the recession. I always work with the business and enjoy the countless facets of my job—I am especially able to make frequent use of my written, analysis and communication skills.

However, my body still worries about creativity and changing the world as I leave my office for the day —both fundamental wishes in me that are critical for getting me feeling whole and complete. Only on this realization did I realize that I had to spend a lot of time channeling these impulses in a way I did not do before. I started to follow my interests more seriously after going through a breakup and moving to a new town.

I started writing more regularly, started to volunteer in a study group in my town and started to work with other people who had to cope with some of the challenges. I tried to authentically cultivate my passions for myself.

Yet my fire is fueling that. When you leave work for the day what makes your heart pound and flutter? What excites you when you're facing an agenda-free Saturday? Upon your time out for the day, how do you get time for these activities?

I will show you why. I will tell you why. These are my suggestions to discover your passion, turn it on, keep it burning and strike the balance between your 9-to-5 tasks:

Think on It

Think about three things, your being, your truth since you have been a child. Was it flute played, oils painted, your family baked macaroons? You may be social and involved and always have enjoyed playing on a football team. How did you stop, when you don't take part in sports or hobbies since childhood?

Perhaps there are improvements to these habits or interests that might be safer for you to realize that you are an adult working. For example, entering a better class will likely be a way of fueled this passion if you enjoyed playing at high school. If you were in a college for your passion, how can a dance lesson for troubled young people be taught? Put your thoughts into it and pursue various hobbies or activities -you may be shocked to find out what makes you tick!

Be True to You

Many times, this is because we feel we need to do these things — because they're trendy, because our peers do it, or because we've got a degree or a special training. Ignoring all the noise, instead of focusing on what you think you should be doing, listen to your intuition moving you in a certain direction. It's all right to do things outside of our box or boxes. It's all right to try something wacky or unusual or unbeatable because it pictures your curiosity. Remember: self-actualization is not people's fun, it is you that needs to find you sometimes before (see tip number one!).

Rediscover Recess

Do you remember having an hour of rest in college to run, play and jump? What are we no longer doing that? Take a day or each week for a little time to play, whether it be for a walk in the woods, a paint-by - the-number tour or dancing in the lounge. A couple of days a week in my calendar I pencil my own customized recess time to make sure I have time to play for my own adult recess. Often I find myself journalizing, singing and making artistic visualizations in YouTube videos. I step outside my door many times and explore my town and find myself in a restaurant that I've never tried before. The truth is that my break is anything in the moment I want it to be. This is when some of my best thoughts, my moments of epiphany, have come to me. Not only is Recess enjoyable, it is important to our personal development.

Consider Making a To-Do List

A commotion list is useful to ensure that you spend time with your passions. Many camps think to - do list interrupt the "at present," but for me a to - do list — which is dynamic and modifiable— holds me on a mission and focuses on my objectives. I never have to jot down (and dream) without a notebook!

Make Your Passion Work for You

You can find yourself having to redeploy your overall plan until you rediscover your passions and realize how important they are for your self-evaluation and the ultimate happiness. Working a full-time job occupies most of the day and it is therefore important to find a time during the week or the weekend where your passion or hobby can be integrated in a way that is both fun and sustainable. If you are a morning man and find that you're on fire before you go to work, that's good. On the opposite, you may want to burn your miniature oil, so that your passion can take place at night. Find a time that works for you and prioritize your passion.

Give it Time

I think we can hear it loud and clear if we take heed of our gut and hear our reality. But passionate searches take time to settle down and grow, particularly if we allow them to sit on the back burner while we try to be more pragmatic. Do not beat yourself; instead, focus on pursuing your passion. It will talk if you listen to it; and if you nurture it, it will grow.

It takes a lot of time and energy to work a day while pursuing and fulfilling your interests, but it is also fundamental human needs— one for economic stability and the other for self-actualization. Many of us— particularly those with a lot of creative drive and entrepreneurial spirit— are critical to a fully enriched life to balance our careers and follow our dreams.

Passion is therefore a personal thing, you and you really love on a journey. Passion means you are laughing, leaping for joy, filling your thoughts and making way for conversations without knowing it. This means something to you, something without which you can exist.

Anything, acts and people can be passionate about. You can enjoy emotions and abstract concepts. For everything you can be passionate for. Many people are more passionate than others, as you probably noticed. Many people put their entire hearts and souls into the things that matters to them and give them 110%. Such people are the kind of people I want to be. They inspire me and make me truly happy to fulfill my passions.

What do you care about? I asked myself this question when I started to write this blog. After all, without first speaking of what I am passionate, I couldn't read very well. Honestly, a lot of things I'm curious about. I'm a people who mean so much to me, optimistic. I'm passionate about some issues, including equality between men and women and animal rights. I'm intrigued by things like books, films, and art that fascinate and inspire me. Nevertheless, writing is one of the things which most stands out in my mind when I hear the word passion. I love writing.-I love to write. I do this as many times as I can. I love it, man. In my house, I have high shelves of newspapers and spiral-bound notebooks. There are novels, poems and a few fragments of ideas on my computer.

I've spent a considerable amount of time online writing since I began this blog-something that I found I love to do. I used to love to write in my journal, to bring all my emotions into those pages, but I found that I love to share the work I have done as I do. I used to be scared of writing anything that I wrote, but the older I get, the more I want to share my words with anyone who is readable. I am both overwhelmed and frightened by a fire, because I was never an open person. I used to lock my childhood newspapers, hide them from my parents, sometimes even sleeping under my pillow. I still have all sorts of passwords on my phone, frustrated friends and family that sometimes want to just use the machine and find out that it is locked up. I am still afraid to put myself completely there in some ways, but every day I get stronger when I let go and really pursue my passion for writing in a more public way.

It's not always simple passions. We may feel strongly and love it with all our might, but it won't easily come to us. Some of life's best things take a lot of toil and effort. Some of the best things in life take bravery and a drive beyond limits. My passion for me is to read. It's the one thing that I always did, and probably the one thing I'll keep doing all my life. It's not always easy to do, however much I like it, and it definitely isn't always easy to share it with other people. I will spend a little time today about why I develop my passion— and how you can cultivate it. Regardless of what you want to do, you have to focus on it if you want to do it as well as possible. You must get to grips with new things and push yourself. Here are my thoughts about how to take advantage of your passion for life:

How to Cultivate Your Passion

Narrow your vision. You can get excited about something if you're anything like me and want to soak in every little bit of it. For starters, I get very excited when I think of writing. I want a novel, poems and journals, posts, and journal entries. I want to read. I want to do everything. It's a great feeling that I want to dive into something, but one of the best things I can say to develop your Passion is: narrow your focus. It may be so tempting to try to do all and anything you want, but if you do, it will overwhelm you and possibly you won't do much. Start small. Small start. Find out what is most important to you and null in it. You can always expand your dream in the future, but start tight to achieve the best results. Concentration is so important and when you get excited about something, it can actually slip away. Make a list of the stuff you love about your passion when you feel completely lost and don't know where to start. You will soon discover what's important for you and you can then collect and concentrate on this knowledge.

Integrate it into your life. Passionate about something? Don't leave it in a corner of your house or apartment and hide it from the world. I used to say I was a writer because I was sitting at home in my apartment typing away on my computer. Yes, I was a writer, but I was a writer in hiding. I wanted to live this very different life -- a positive life -- and yet I would sit alone and write most of the time. I still do this today, but I also work hard to share what I write with the world. I'm blogging three days a week. I'm writing guest posts for others' sites. I'm online on social media sites trying to get the word out about what I'm writing about. I'm telling friends and family about my blogs. It can be hard work (and, in my case, pretty intimidating) to share what you're passionate about with others, but the more you share and put yourself out there, the more opportunities you'll have to make your passion a big part of your life.

Work as hard as you can. Just as nothing good has ever been achieved without ambition, without hard work nothing successful has ever been accomplished. You have to work on it if you love it. You must do so as often as you can (without worrying too much), and as many different ways as you can. As much as hard work can get awful, all the effort you put in it will be worth it if you are very passionate about something. For example, writing my blog posts and answering comments, e-mails, etc. takes me a lot of time. Little time. Less time. Sometimes this takes away something else that I could do, such as hanging out with friends or simply putting a good book. Even if I love to do it, sometimes it's hard to do it. But what are you sure of? It really needs to be at the end of the day. I cannot help being filled with joy and gratitude when I get an email from someone in my box telling me that I have changed my life. This feeling can't be compared, and it pays off every hour of hard labor.

Make it tons of fun. Occasionally, when people love something, they get so centered on it that they lose sight of everything's enjoyable. It can quickly be recalled if you get so lost in something that you can think of little else. There's something really great fun! Go behind your excitement and find out how to make it enjoyable. You can forget what inspired you in the first place if you become too focused. There must be a way to make it fun, regardless of why you feel passionate about your passion. In some situations, you have to be a little imaginative, but you can always find it even more fun to do something you love. One idea is to find a way to integrate others into your passion. There are probably others who enjoy it, whatever you do. Search for them and start a club or band. Even if you don't have people around you who love what you do, you can find a way that they can enjoy sharing with them.

Be innovative and creative. When you spend time with what you feel excited about, consider two things: creativity and growth. You are already motivated and willing to talk, reflect and work on your passion. You must move this to the next level now. You must be innovative and creative. You have to think about how to get out of the comfort zone and try new things. The wheel here you don't have to reinvent. You just need to find a different way to do stuff— which could mean something else to you. I just wanted to write, for example. For as long as I can remember, I've done it every day. I chose to share it one day, however. This was not the most intellectual revelation, and it probably didn't really mean all that much to my blog's early readers, but it was HUGE to me. It changed life. I broke off my habits and got out of my comfort zone. It affected me. It was hard and still terrifying (and is!), but worth it. Everything I love to do has made me happier and, above all, has kept me responsible for what I do. This makes me want to work harder and more creative than I would be if I was still in the middle of the papers on my desktop. I know there are people who writing. You can find ways to break your own style. There must be no crazy thing that never has been done before. All it has to do is pushing you and inspiring you to be even more enthusiastic about what you do.

Share your ideas with others. You should be mindful that, following my example above, sharing what you like with others is very important. It may be difficult to do (many people have unusual stuff that they love and they like me don't want to share with us), but it is one of the best ways to develop your passion. I was afraid nobody would want to read my blog when I started blogging first, or worse, people could read it and hate it. I never thought I would have the sort of positive reviews I regularly get. I never thought some of the people reading my blog would become some of my life's most important people. The blog has changed my life in so many ways, and I would never have seen some of the big things that I've had over the past year if I didn't take a leap of faith and get out. It still frightens me when I think of people reading my blogs, sometimes, but I still do. Even when I'm scared, I force myself to be more than I know I can be. And what are you sure of? It's cool. It feels good to break from my field of comfort and receive some positive reviews. It is good to tell my readers and to know that someone is reading and taking care of what I have to say somewhere out there. Maybe you don't want to express your enthusiasm, but this is a great way to take advantage of what you like.

Give yourself a break. As much as I love writing and I want to do it endlessly, one of the best ways I have found to use my passion is to take a break. I was online seven days a week when I started blogging, and almost every day I blogged a new post. I've been good internally, I've been super excited and the pressure has grown as numbers of readers. I feel like I've been writing all the time and I've been overwhelmed. Instead I knew I needed a break. I have created a new routine so I only post three days a week and suddenly, rather than being pushed into, I felt more relaxed and more willing to really enjoy writing. Keep this in mind as the passion is being explored. You don't have to do this 24 hours a day as much as it does to you. A break can be taken. You can actually take several breaks. And, frankly, you must do so. It can be tempting to focus endlessly on something, but one of the best ways to maximize your creativity is to breathe in and step back once in a while. You will come back cool and even more pumped about the things you enjoy doing.

In particular, I'm all about love. I think everyone must be so excited to do it or talk about it or share it with others. I believe that they should all be so excited. Many don't have this — but that doesn't mean that they can't. I truly believe he or she is passionate about almost everybody is. It is only a question of finding out what it is. When you have come to it (and you may already know) use the above ideas to help you reach the next level of your passion. You can walk the path of passion one step at a time and get so much closer to what you want to do.

Chapter 15
A Simple Equation That Can Help You Discover Your Passion

Such men are all familiar to us. Those who seem to be born to do what they are doing. Those who can't wait every day for work. We wouldn't do anything else, no matter whether they were artists, actors or Wall Street stock brokers. This passion helps them to cope with their pure, unrestrained excitement in their life.

When did they get to the job? And how can we go about them?

Let's first get one thing out of the way: "Follow your heart" is incorrect. It doesn't happen because of the desires of certain individuals that they are expected to read, play golf or research the stars.

The cultivation of passion

Reflect the claims of Cal Newport. The author of four books on love is a computer scientist and Newport. He's not buying into the philosophy of "follow your passion." Newport says, "There's no unique love waiting for you to discover in an interview with Joshua Fields Millburn. Therefore, let's explore an equation that I built with this in mind: Passion is something cultivated.'

(Curiosity + engagement) x time = passion

We're curious to begin with. We're attracted from a young age to things we're interested in and when we get older, we can hone into something that really appeals to us.

It's here that most of us are trapped because we're scared of "true" options. But note, what Newport said: "There's no specific passion waiting to discover you." In other words, there is no "wrong" option because there's no "right" option either. Roll it up and pick an interest.

We acquire knowledge about this subject, which needs more interest, when we have selected something.

The importance of the company we keep

We also need to meet other people interested in our interests, apart from acquiring knowledge in the traditional way. That's two things. Second, detailed knowledge of individuals is easier to collect than from static media. Furthermore, the social engagement between our values only reinforces our commitment and boosts this passion.

There is an explanation why parents do not want their children hanging out with the bad crowd. "People's lives," says Anthony Robbins, a world-renowned life coach, "are often a direct reflection of the expectations of their peer group." What Robbins is saying is that we set the bar for our lives based on how those around us set theirs. There is no one to compare with or share our ideas and experiences when choosing the violin as the passion to cultivate, but we don't hang out with other musicians. On the other side, we meet people who are our mentors and colleagues when we join the music scene. You are motivating us and keeping us to account.

Engagement, engagement, engagement

But without clear interaction all this interest and social context would be meaningless. There, the formula of love really revives. Regularly and over and over again, our curiosity makes it easier, clearer and more interesting. The more fascinating it is, the more enthusiasm it creates.

"Whatever we focus on actually wires our neurons," Kare Anderson says. Anderson says. "Whether you pay attention to it— or not— it has an enormous impact on how you perceive and experience the world." It takes months and years to develop our interests and to connect. The passion is gradually rooted in our minds during this gestation period. When we are in design, we start to see the connection between our art and the message that we are trying to convey. If we are in accounting, the balance sheet and cash flow statement continue to be inter-related.

Continuous engagement always encourages our curiosity and social involvement. The chosen interest and the stuff around it have to be continually intrigued, deeper and deeper down the rabbit holes. We also often have to meet new people, compare notes, inspire and answer for each other.

We have been trapped because, "further to your passion" is incorrect. what this passion formula tells us is intense. Over time, passion is only interest and devotion. The reality is that we are the master, and the follower is love.

Now, go and "discover" your passion!

We were all enthusiastic graduates. We are curious about all around us in the world. We wanted to speak, crawl and walk. We wanted to. See a kid take the first leap and learn on the basis of enthusiasm. Listen to a player until they are ready to perform a challenging piece. Watch a snowboardsman repeatedly try a new trick — that doesn't give up persistence and passion.

In many situations, school is associated with pacing guides, required curriculum, grade standards, bell schedules, grades and testing teaching. You're unable to experience this kind of passion at school. The teacher or the authorities are the ones in charge in such circumstances. The teacher tends to be responsible for the learning. However, to truly learn something, the student must possess and guide their learning.

I thought about who I was as a student and focused on teaching and doing work that is insufficient for myself. So that I could get through "through" school, I learned the game from school and "do" school.

Chapter 16
Be The Master Of Your Time

Do you often feel that you're short of time? Say you scheduled three tasks for today. You start the day full of energy to tackle those three tasks. At the end of the day, you have barely completed the first task because there were other things that demanded your attention.

Way too many people suffer from a disease called procrastination. I'll admit, there are times where I've fallen victim to procrastination too. I used to believe that procrastination was an excuse we used when we're either afraid or too lazy to do anything.

Procrastination usually arises when people fear or dread, or have anxiety about, the important task awaiting them. To rid themselves of this negative feeling, people procrastinate. Some of the same attributes can be applied to poor time management. It's not that you don't have time it's that you're either wasting time (by avoiding the thing that needs to be done and using the time to do something else) or not making the most of the time you have (not planning accordingly in order to complete important tasks).

The first thing you need to recognize in time management is **you have the same amount of time as everyone in the world**. Steve Jobs, Bill Gates, Warren Buffett, Tiger Woods, Michael Jordan, and every person in this world has 24 hours every day and 365 days a year, just like you do. Time is not a limited commodity because it is always there, unfolding every second before you. There is no time to manage. Time is just what it is. You cannot arrange your "time," make an hour shorter or longer, or make time faster or slower.

The concept of time is an artificial human construct. It is a system of measurement invented by Man to give meaning to what is before us. Centuries, decades, years, months, weeks, days, hours, minutes, seconds, and milliseconds — these are just terms that we created to assert control over the fluidity of time.

In addition, it is a decent creation too. The construct of time has helped us establish order and understanding among all humans as we lead our lives in an orderly fashion. When you say, "Let's meet at 9am this Friday," your friends understand you because we have a common understanding of how time works, as demarcated by weeks/days/hours/minutes/seconds.

But in reality, time is just what it is. You do not need more time nor do you have a lack of time. Time is always there. You have all the time before you.

Reframing the problem in Time Management

Nonetheless, you need to carry out tasks by the end of every day. The skills and procedures needed for conducting these tasks are better to ensure they are done within the specified time period. The mission and self-management are what you need to know and not time management.

Here I am giving you a quote from the author of Getting Things Done by David Allen: "It is just time that you can't manage. "Time management" is therefore a mislabeled issue that is not likely to be an effective approach. The center of the system required to manage what you do is your behavior over time, and to determine the results and physical actions needed. "The scope of the task management is so broad that it cannot be addressed in just one article. I start by sharing the basic task management theory, followed by articles based on this definition. I'll also discuss the concepts and strategies you may apply to your job and self-management.

Due to the fact that time management is an all-around concept, in this article and other posts on this blog I shall use it interchangeably with project management. You know however what I mean—"time management" is a misnomer, and we really are looking at project and self-management.

Two Pillars of Time Management: Effectiveness and Efficiency

The core of time management can break into two parts: **effectiveness** and **efficiency**.

1. **Effectiveness means doing the important.** This means prioritizing, focusing and saying no to things that are not in line with your major goals for life. It means making things your focus.
2. **Efficiency means to produce maximum output with minimum wasted input**. It ensures that it is possible to do things quickly and precise. Improved production with the same or less time and energy expenditure.

Effectiveness

Most people attribute inefficiencies in their time management when the real chance lies in being successful. Two measures can be made to be successful. Firstly, the important tasks can be carried out in less important tasks. Secondly, the main aspects of the important tasks are centered. Prioritization is the nature of performance. Experience every one of us in turn.

1: Do the important tasks first

If you focus on your projects in order of priority, success takes place. If you don't often have enough time for anything (exercise, relationships), you didn't give it enough attention. You wanted to do other stuff about it, and so you "don't have enough time" to do it. Perhaps you are not sure of this particular activity's relative importance to other issues with which you are associated. Perhaps you're stuck in doing things that are meaningless.

For example, you might have wanted to go to the fitness center after work, but work requires you to do it. Here, you have made your job more important than exercise. You may have easily weighed the benefits of late work over late learning and concluded that the latter was a better choice than the latter. The attention was on the urgent nature of the work, but you can exercise later.

It's your personal choice to do what you have done, whatever it's. For advance time management, it is important to own your choices. Others spend their day at random events like watching TV, talk and lazy web surfing. We look back at the end of the day and wonder where their day is. Is their effectiveness a problem? Definitely. Absolutely. We have chosen to prioritize meaningless things for what they really care about.

I would like to ask here, "What is important to me? These are the most important tasks I could do in my life for the tasks I am doing now?"

Step #2: Do the important steps within the task

Let's look at the second step, which focuses on the main aspects of the project.

You say you should make a presentation at a school and have prioritized it on your list for other activities. Furthermore, you spend most of your time on less important tasks when working on the report. You use 50 percent of your time to change minute information such as matching font colors and fixing text alignment on every slide, instead of focusing on content quality.

Now I don't mean it's not important to look the materials professional and consistently. I did my fair share of presentations, at least several hundred at school and at work.

But the purpose and the aim of this mission should be clearly explained. The purpose of this paper (let's say) is to achieve a grade A. Your content, execution and audience participation constitute the components of the class. The layout of the diapas can influence the perception of the public at an intangible level.

Since the content and execution are the essence of this presentation mission, not the layout. There is a gap between 10% and 80% of your development time. These little things won't matter if your slide design looks awful at the start. The more presentations I have, the more time I spend on material, the arrangement of ideas, my presentation and future questions, rather than minor details like formatting, looking and feeling.

I recall how I spent so much time on design and coding when I first took part in college meetings, which did not make any major difference in the big picture. I will put my distribution work away, which is how I would place it on my chaos list at the end of the day. It was a huge mistake, because I finally had little or no time to work on my speech and delivery.

Nowadays, depending on the people I meet, my presentations can be a simple black text on a white background. Naturally, I'll work in design when I meet a crowd that sees design as part of the product. Ultimately, it restricts itself to giving priority to the steps involved.

Efficiency

Performance, that is, quickly and accurately doing things, has less of an effect than performance. That is because the time and the degree to which we can function within our human ability is minimal.

Say you've got a typing file. It is a 6,000-word document that you wrote on paper already and must be printed out. The work is done in 100 minutes with a typing speed of 60 WPM (Words per minute). You will finish the job in 92 minutes if you try to type faster at 65 WPM, which shaves your original time off eight minutes which is great, but not much in the larger scheme of things. This means that you make no more mistakes with the speed increases!

On the other hand, it allows you to improve your performance (first to take on the right tasks). An example of flexibility here is to type the report directly into your computer instead of writing it on paper and then moving it to your computer, which is a further step. A pen scanner can be used to check the text even though it may not be as good as the first one. It is subject to error. You can even assign or outsource information to someone who does the job at no cost to you. If you are in a higher position where there is a chronic lack of time, it helps to move your tasks for a fee since you have much more time savings than the price of recruiting.

Returning to the example above, instead of writing it on paper, you can type the report directly in your computer and forward it to the computer which will provide a further phase. You can use a pen scanner to check the text, although it is not as good as the previous one. It is even possible to assign or outsource the entry to someone who does the job at no cost to your time.

It is definitely important to improve performance, but we should ensure we are successful before we strive for efficiency. In general, the success of our assignments and changes in strategy means paradigm shifts. Rate, action and accuracy are improved by performance.

Today, many people make the error of focusing on productivity and think that is time management. Quality in order to maximize our performance must come before quality. Such a plan allows you, instead of being literally blown up by whomever events to you, to arrange your day according to your needs and expectations.

www.ingramcontent.com/pod-product-compliance
Lightning Source LLC
Chambersburg PA
CBHW021434210526
45463CB00002B/508